CHRISTMAS FEASTS

by

LORNA J. SASS

THE METROPOLITAN MUSEUM OF ART
and
IRENA CHALMERS COOKBOOKS, INC.
New York

Contents

ISBN # 0-941034-01-1; Library of Congress Catalog Card # 81-68835
MMA edition ISBN # 0-87099-281-3
© 1981 by Lorna J. Sass.
All rights reserved. Printed and published in the United States of America
by Irena Chalmers Cookbooks, Inc.

For Steve, who makes it feel like Christmas in July

Acknowledgments

Hearty thanks to Irena Chalmers for inviting me to write a book on such a fascinating subject, to Jean Atcheson for superb and sensitive editing, to Alden Rockwell for industrious picture research, to Mary Ann Joulwan for uniting pictures and text with such care, to Michele Urvater for assistance in recipe testing, to Louis Szathmary for permission to quote from a cookery manuscript in his collection, to Michael Smith for providing a constant source of inspiration on the subject of fine English food, and to J. Audrey Ellison for a careful reading of the text. Heartiest thanks go to Stephen C. Chamberlain for providing constant support and companionship, for patiently editing the text and for cheerfully washing so many dishes.

Adapted recipes for *Goos in Sawse Madame, Crustade Lombard, Brede, Hippocras, A Dyschefull of Snowe,* and *Artichoke Puding* are reprinted, with permission, from my books *To the King's Taste/To the Queen's Taste,* published by The Metropolitan Museum of Art, 1975/1976.

A NOTE ON THE RECIPES

I feel it is of primary importance for readers to see the original recipes which served as the basis for my modern-day adaptations. All of the historical recipes have therefore been provided, and the antiquated spelling (or lack thereof) has been faithfully reproduced. In the old English recipes, I have added some short explanations or translations in square brackets; the Roman recipes, originally in Latin, have all been given in contemporary English translations. Notes and some suggestions for further reading appear on pages 82-83.

You may mail-order all of the unusual herbs and spices needed in the recipes from Aphrodisia, 28 Carmine Street, New York, NY 10014. Whenever feasible, suitable substitutes have been suggested in the ingredients lists. When testing the recipes, I have sometimes thought it advisable to deviate somewhat from the original in order to accommodate differences in ingredients and tastes. In comparing the original recipes against my adaptations, you may come up with alternative interpretations. I hope that you will experiment with your ideas and have a very good time preparing and eating these unusually delicious foods.

L.J.S.

Introduction

"He has more to do than the ovens in England at Christmas," goes the old Italian saying. The goal of *Christmas Feasts* is to open those historic oven doors and serve forth rich lore, delicious recipes and festive menus for preparing five unforgettable Yuletide feasts.

The book begins with the celebration of a Roman Saturnalia banquet, for in the Saturnalia many historians see the pagan roots of Christmas. By the Middle Ages, a thousand years later, Christmas had become a legendary celebration highlighted by the presentation of a garlanded boar's head to the harmony of Christmas carols. During the 17th century, old Father Christmas had a rough time: celebrations were actually outlawed in Puritan England, but as we well know, "Roast Beef and brave Plum-porridge" survived their temporary banishment.

The Yuletide season in the 18th century abounded with larger-than-life pageantry: there are records of 800-pound puddings and pies filled with all the fowl in the barnyard. With the 19th century came the first Christmas cards and the tree itself, as well as Dickens's unforgettable Cratchits, "steeped in sage and onion to the eyebrows."

Light has always been a symbol common to Christmas celebrations. It is no accident that Christmas falls at the time of the winter solstice, that period in the Northern Hemisphere when the sun is so far south that it seems to disappear altogether, leaving the earth in almost total darkness. Then, as gradually as it vanishes, the sun appears again, warming and lighting the earth, bringing with it the promise of new crops and a new year. It is in this recurrent drama, the rebirth of the sun, that people from earliest times have found cause for celebration.

In these celebrations, the color green has played as predominant a role as has light itself. The persistent greenness of holly, ivy and pine has made these plants natural symbols of enduring life during those long wintry months filled with deathlike darkness. Since at least Roman times, evergreens have been brought indoors to celebrate the season, and by the 15th century it was the custom at Christmas for "every man's house, as also the parish churches" to be "decked with . . . ivy, bays, and whatsoever the season of the year afforded to be green."

Enveloped within the mysterious powers of greenness and light—the two most prominent features of any Christmas tree—are the seeds of that special holiday created to celebrate the birth of Christ. While breaking bread with loved ones and while making your way through this book, I hope you will take pleasure in watching those seeds grow—by the light of the flame under your pot, the candle on your dining-room table and the blaze of the plum pudding.

Merry Christmas!

LORNA J. SASS
Feasts Unlimited
New York City

A Roman Saturnalia Banquet

*A great order of the ages is born anew. Now
the virgin, now the reign of Saturn, comes again;
now a new progeny descends from heaven.*

VIRGIL, The Eclogues

With these remarkably prophetic words, the poet Virgil (70-19 B.C.) described the Saturnalia, the merry festival that was the traditional culmination of the ancient Roman year. Named for Saturnus, the Roman god of seeds and sowing, the celebration probably began to commemorate the end of the autumn sowing season in southern Italy, a time of brief respite from the yearly round of farm chores, a time to pause and exchange good will with neighbors and friends.

"All Rome seemed to go mad on this holiday," exclaimed the Roman statesman Seneca, describing the Saturnalia. Beginning around December 17, all work was suspended for seven days and Romans took to the streets with carnival-like abandon shouting, *"Io Saturnalia!"* Slaves were free to do and say what they pleased and a mock king was chosen ruler. Characteristics of what was to become Christmas were already in evidence: halls festooned with laurel leaves, gifts exchanged—often little dolls made of clay or dough—and small wax tapers lit as protection against the hovering spirits of darkness.

The week-long festival reached its peak on or about December 25, a day set aside for special reverence to the sun. Influenced by the Persian religion of Mithraism, the Romans celebrated *Dies solis invicti nati*, The Day of the Birth of the Unconquered Sun, the moment in its cycle when the sun was at its nadir, poised to offer a bountifully increasing gift of daylight, so essential to man and all growing things.

The Saturnalia always struck me as a holiday well worth celebrating, but for years I had been discouraged about the idea of making a Roman banquet. The recipes called for such unusual combinations of ingredients, and I couldn't think how to duplicate *liquamen*, the ubiquitous fermented fish sauce which the Romans used instead of salt. A few years ago, after doing much reading about exotic Roman dining, I was inspired to take ladle in hand and offer my taste buds some new sensations. A colleague, Michele Urvater, suggested that I use *nuoc mam* as a substitute for *liquamen*. This salty fermented fish sauce, a popular ingredient in Southeast Asian cooking, is often available at oriental groceries; failing *nuoc mam*, soy sauce may also be used with satisfactory results, particularly if two anchovy fillets are mashed and combined with each cup of soy sauce and the mixture is left to stand for a few days before use.

The Romans used spices in a very provocative and, to our tastes, curious manner. For example, pepper was particularly prized and often used as a garnish, much as we might use paprika or confectioners' sugar today (see the recipe for Patina of Pears). Some of the more complicated recipes contain so many different flavors blended together that presumably no single flavor was expected to predominate. In fact, keeping the diner in the dark about the ingredients of a dish was actually a goal of the skilled Roman cook. "At table no one will know what he is eating" is the bold claim made proudly at the end of one Roman recipe.[1]*

The major and virtually unique source of Roman recipes is Apicius' *De re coquinaria*, "Of Things Culinary."[2] The original author of this cookbook is believed to have been M. Gavius Apicius, who lived in the early part of the 1st century A.D. He was reputed to have had an extremely refined palate and the culinary skills to satisfy it. The only text of this work that has survived is actually a compilation of various Roman recipes from the 1st to the 4th centuries A.D., some presumably from the original Apicius and others from following centuries.

When a Roman guest arrived for a Saturnalia feast, his feet were washed by a slave. He was then announced by the *nomenclator* and directed to his place on one of the three long couches which surrounded a low, central table. Each couch, or *triclinium*, was divided into three sections by cushions; each diner would recline on the couch, facing the table and resting his left elbow on one of the cushions. Before the meal began, gold-embroidered napkins were spread before the diners and *ministratores* circulated with bowls of perfumed water for hand-washing—the right hand was the primary eating utensil, occasionally aided by a spoon. Forks were not used for eating.

How many courses did the reclining diners enjoy during the course of a complete Roman banquet? It depends on who is doing the counting, but most scholars agree that the Roman dinner was divided into three main parts: the appetizer or *gustatio* (raw and cooked vegetables, seafood and egg dishes); the main course or *mensae primae* (a wide variety of roasted and boiled meats); and the dessert course or *mensae secundae* (fruit, raw and cooked, and a range of sweets such as cakes and custards).

With the first course, *mulsam*, a sweet drink made by adding honey to wine, was served. During the remainder of the meal, guests would be offered a variety of wines, both resined and unresined. Great pottery *amphorae* would be uncorked and the wine poured through a funnel strainer into a large mixing bowl. In this *cratera* the wine was mixed with water and often cooled with snow.

The pages of Roman literature are punctuated with detailed descriptions of both modest and excessive banqueting fare. Here is a menu that falls somewhere in between, and is eminently suitable for a Roman Saturnalia Banquet in the 1980s.

*Notes to each chapter may be found on pages 82-83.

A Roman Saturnalia Banquet

GUSTATIO

Mussels in Liquamen   Cabbage Salad with Coriander   Lentils with Chestnuts

MENSAE PRIMAE

Pork Fricassee with Apricots   Chicken Fronto

MENSAE SECUNDAE

Patina of Pears   Honey-Fried Stuffed Dates

Rose Wine

Serve *mulsam* with the *gustatio*, red or white wine with the entrées, and rose wine (see recipe) with dessert.

Mussels in Liquamen

Apicius' cookbook offers many interesting recipes for seafood, although in some instances it's difficult to know precisely which fish he intends. In the following recipe for Salt Fish Without Fish, one of Apicius' numerous "trick foods," the choice of "fish" is obviously left up to the cook: "Cook liver, grind and add pepper and liquamen or salt. Add oil. Use hare, kid, lamb, or chicken-liver: and mould into a fish in a small mould if liked. Sprinkle virgin oil over it."

The passum *mentioned in the mussel recipe was a sweet wine made from raisins. The combination of ingredients in this recipe is extremely successful with the steamed mussels.*

**4 pounds mussels, scrubbed and
  bearded**
1 large leek
**2 tablespoons liquamen (nuoc mam
  or slightly less soy sauce
  flavored with anchovies)**
**2 tablespoons passum (Malaga wine
  does very nicely)**
½ teaspoon bruised cumin seed
**½ teaspoon (dry) summer or winter
  savory**
¼ cup dry white wine
½ cup water

Place the cleaned mussels in a large heavy pot that has a lid.

Remove the green tail and root of the leek, and coarsely chop the white. Place the chopped leek in a strainer and run water over it to remove any sand. Pat dry.

In a bowl, combine the chopped leek with the remaining ingredients. Pour the mixture over the mussels. Cover the pot and cook over very high heat about 2 minutes, or just until the mussels open. Do not overcook or the mussels will become rubbery.

Place the mussels in a large serving bowl and pour the sauce on top. Serve hot or at room temperature.

MUSSELS IN LIQUAMEN

Mix liquamen, chopped leek, cumin, passum, savory, and wine, dilute the mixture with water, and cook the mussels in it.

Apicius
The Roman Cookery Book, IX, ix

Cabbage Salad with Coriander

Makes 8 servings

In his Natural History, *Pliny (23-79 A.D.) has a good deal to say about the varieties of cabbage known to his contemporaries. Among the types he mentions are the cabbage from Cumae, with broad short leaves and an open, spreading head; one from Aricia, not very high, with many tough leaves, and with shoots coming out from under almost every leaf; the cabbage from Pompeii, tall, with a stalk thin at the root; and the Sabellian cabbage, with very thick curly leaves and a thin stem.*

You might like to experiment with this recipe if a variety of cabbages is available to you; however, I can vouch for the goodness of this cabbage salad when made with the common round-headed variety.

1 medium-size cabbage
3 tablespoons liquamen (nuoc mam, or slightly less soy sauce flavored with anchovies)
½ cup olive oil
½ cup dry white wine
1 teaspoon bruised cumin seeds

Garnishes: the white of 1 large leek, cleaned and coarsely chopped; 3-4 tablespoons chopped fresh coriander (Chinese parsley or cilantro);
freshly ground pepper;
additional cumin seeds (optional)

Remove the outer leaves of the cabbage. Rinse the cabbage and cut it into quarters. Steam the cabbage in about an inch of boiling water for 5 to 7 minutes, or until the leaves are tender, but still crisp. Drain the cabbage, then shred it as for cole slaw.

In a small bowl, prepare the dressing by combining the liquamen, oil, wine and cumin. Add just enough dressing to coat the cabbage.

Garnish with chopped leek, coriander, ground pepper and additional cumin (if desired). Adjust the seasonings. Serve warm or chilled.

LENTILS WITH CHESTNUTS

[Boil the lentils.] Take a new saucepan and put in the carefully cleaned chestnuts. Add water and a little cooking soda. Put on the fire to cook. [Meanwhile], put in the mortar pepper, cumin, coriander seed, mint, rue, asafoetida root, and pennyroyal; pound. Moisten with vinegar, add honey and liquamen, blend with vinegar and pour over the cooked chestnuts. Add oil, bring to the boil. When it is boiling well, stir. [Mix with the lentils.] Taste: if something is missing, add it. When you have put it in the serving-dish, add best oil.

APICIUS
The Roman Cookery Book, V, ii, 2

Lentils with Chestnuts

The marriage of lentils to chestnuts is a happy one, but the wide array of flavorings in this recipe certainly reveals the Roman penchant for avoiding simple, straightforward pairings.

The Romans loved spices and put a great deal of their energies into obtaining them through exploration and trade, in large part with the Arabs. The habit of using exotic seasonings then spread throughout the vast Roman empire—even as far as Britain.

1 cup dried lentils
1½ cups dried chestnuts (see note)
¼ teaspoon black peppercorns
½ teaspoon whole cumin seed
¼ teaspoon coriander seed
½ teaspoon dried mint
⅛ teaspoon dried rue
⅛ teaspoon ground asafoetida
½ teaspoon dried pennyroyal
2 tablespoons liquamen (nuoc mam, or slightly less soy sauce flavored with anchovies)
2 tablespoons wine vinegar
1 tablespoon honey
1-2 tablespoons olive oil
Garnishes: additional olive oil; bay leaves

Rinse the lentils and then the chestnuts. Place each in a separate pot, cover them with cold water and bring to the boil. Remove both pots from the heat. Cover the pots and let the lentils and chestnuts sit for 2 hours. Then simmer them until soft, uncovered, replenishing water as needed.

Drain the lentils and chestnuts. (If you wish this dish to be soupy, reserve some of the cooking liquids. In this case, you will probably want to add larger quantities of the herbs and spices. I prefer to drain off all the liquid, but the recipe is not at all clear on the matter.) Set aside.

Combine the herbs and spices and pound them to a powder in a mortar, or use an electric spice mill. Place the lentils, chestnuts, ground spices and remaining ingredients in a large heavy pot, stirring to distribute the flavors. Cook, covered, over low heat for 30 minutes. (Placing your pot on an asbestos pad prevents scorching the bottom of the mixture.) Check seasoning. "If something is missing, add it."

Place the mixture in a serving bowl. Add additional olive oil on top and garnish decoratively with bay leaves. Serve hot or at room temperature.

NOTE: If fresh chestnuts are in season, you may prefer to use them. In this case, roast about 50 chestnuts by making a ½-inch slit in each (to avoid bursting) and bake them on a cookie sheet in a 400-degree oven for about 15 minutes, or until the chestnuts are soft and the peels slip off easily. Add the peeled chestnuts as directed in paragraph 3.

Pork Fricassee with Apricots

Apicius includes recipes for most parts of the pig: the liver, stomach (stuffed), trotters, shoulder and leg. The successful combination of meat and fruit evident in this recipe is a characteristic we nowadays associate with Middle Eastern food; it may well be that the Romans were introduced to this dish one afternoon while trading spices with the Persians.

3½-pound shoulder or loin of pork, trimmed (or, if you have 5 cups pork already cooked, dice it and skip the roasting instructions)

2 tablespoons olive oil

2 tablespoons chopped shallot

3 teaspoons liquamen (nuoc mam, or slightly less soy sauce flavored with anchovies)

1 cup dry red wine

½ teaspoon peppercorns

1 teaspoon each, dried mint, cumin seed and dill weed

1 tablespoon honey

¼ cup passum (Malaga wine does very nicely)

1 teaspoon wine vinegar

12 sweet ripe apricots, stoned and halved (or 1-pound can of apricots, drained)

3-4 tablespoons ground sweet biscuit or shortbread crumbs

Garnish: freshly ground pepper

PORK FRICASSEE WITH APRICOTS

Put in the saucepan oil, liquamen, wine, chop in dry shallot, add diced shoulder of pork cooked previously. When all this is cooked, pound pepper, cumin, dried mint, and dill. Moisten with honey, liquamen, passum, a little vinegar, and some of the cooking liquor; mix well. Add the stoned apricots. Bring to the boil, and let it boil until done. Crumble pastry to bind. Sprinkle with pepper and serve.

APICIUS
The Roman Cookery Book, IV, iii, 6

Preheat oven to 375 degrees.

Set the pork in an oiled roasting pan or on a rack and roast at 375 degrees for 1 hour and 45 minutes. Remove the pork from the oven and cut it into large dice, trimming off any fat. Set aside.

Heat the oil in a large skillet. Add the shallots and cook for 1 to 2 minutes. Add 2 teaspoons of the liquamen and the wine; bring to the boil and reduce the liquid slightly. Add the diced pork and simmer for about 15 minutes, stirring occasionally.

Meanwhile, combine the spices and herbs and pound them to a powder in a mortar, or use an electric spice grinder. In a small saucepan, combine the ground spices with the honey, remaining teaspoon of liquamen, passum, wine vinegar, and ½ cup of the wine-based liquid in which the pork is simmering.

Bring to a boil. Add the apricots and simmer for 10 minutes. Add the biscuit crumbs, stirring with a small whisk until the sauce thickens slightly. Adjust seasonings.

Using a slotted spoon, lift the pork from the remaining cooking liquid and place in a serving bowl. Pour the sauce over the pork and garnish with freshly ground pepper.

Chitken Fronto

Unlike our chefs, with their habit of reducing wine during the cooking process, the Romans preferred to reduce the wine before adding it to the other ingredients. In this delicious chicken in the style of Fronto (Fronto is believed to have been the author of agricultural writings), defrutum *is used for the sauce. According to writers of the period,* defrutum *was must (unfermented grape juice) boiled down to at least half of its original volume. I have used reduced unsweetened grape juice (preferably white) with excellent results.*

**4-pound chicken, skinned and
  chopped into small pieces**
3 tablespoons olive oil
**1 large leek, cleaned and coarsely
  chopped**
**1 tablespoon each, minced fresh dill
  and coriander**
½ teaspoon dried summer savory
**2 cups defrutum (i.e., 4 cups
  unsweetened grape juice reduced
  to 2)**
**¼ cup liquamen (nuoc mam, or
  slightly less soy sauce
  flavored with anchovies)**
**Garnish: freshly ground black
  pepper**

CHICKEN FRONTO

Brown the chicken, put in a mixture of liquamen and oil to which you add a bouquet of dill, leek, savory, and green coriander; and [cook]. When it is done take it out, place on a serving-dish, sprinkle generously with defrutum, powder with pepper, and serve.

APICIUS
The Roman Cookery Book, VI, ix, 12

Preheat oven to 375 degrees.

In a large skillet, brown the chicken parts in olive oil. Remove the chicken, and sauté the leek in the same olive oil, adding the dill, coriander and savory. Deglaze the pan with ½ cup of the defrutum (bring the liquid to the boil and scrape all the brown bits into it).

Transfer all of the ingredients to a casserole. Add the liquamen. Cover and bake at 375 degrees for 45 minutes, or until the chicken is done.

Just before serving, heat the remaining defrutum to boiling and pour it over the chicken. Garnish with freshly ground pepper and serve.

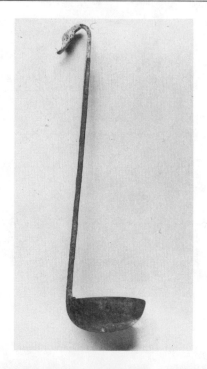

Patina of Pears

Apicius offers a wide range of dishes which he calls "patinas." Almost all of them are bound with eggs although the other ingredients vary considerably: boiled brains with pepper; pureed asparagus with fig-peckers (tiny birds); sea urchins with chickens, boiled greens and almost everything else imaginable.

Serve this recipe for patina of pears in small portions as it is rather rich. The ground-pepper garnish is fascinating and will expand your sense of what is possible.

2 pounds Anjou pears, quartered, cored and peeled
½ cup passum (Malaga wine does very nicely)
½ cup water
¼ teaspoon each, freshly ground pepper and ground cumin
1 tablespoon honey
¼ teaspoon liquamen (nuoc mam, or slightly less soy sauce flavored with anchovies)
1 teaspoon olive oil
2 medium eggs, beaten
Garnish: freshly ground pepper

PATINA OF PEARS

Boil and core pears, pound with pepper, cumin, honey, passum, liquamen, and a little oil. Add eggs to make a patina-mixture, sprinkle with pepper, and serve.

APICIUS
The Roman Cookery Book, IV, ii, 35

Place the pears, passum and water in a heavy saucepan. Cover and simmer over medium heat for 10 minutes, or until the pears are soft. Puree the mixture in a blender or pound it in a mortar.

Combine the puree and the remaining ingredients in the top of a double boiler. Cook over boiling water, stirring constantly, until the mixture thickens. Take care not to let the puree boil or the eggs will curdle.

Place small portions of the puree in cordial glasses or cups. Garnish each portion with a grinding of pepper. Serve warm or chilled.

Honey-Fried Stuffed Dates

Makes 8-10 servings

The Roman delight in food trickery is evident here, in the scheme of replacing the date pits with delicious nuts. This dessert provides interesting extremes of salty and sweet, smooth and crunchy.

20 large dates
20 filbert nuts or about 60 pine nuts (pignolia)
Sea salt
¼ cup (or more) honey

Carefully cut open one side of each date and remove the pit. Place a filbert nut or about 3 pine nuts in the center of each date and squeeze the slit edges together until they meet.

Sprinkle some salt on a sheet of waxed paper. Roll each date lightly in the salt. Spread the salt evenly over each date with your fingers, brushing off the excess. In a small saucepan, heat the honey just until it begins to foam. Simmer over a *very* low flame and gently drop in a few dates, roll them over, and then lift them out with a slotted spoon. (Be careful that the honey does not get so hot that it caramelizes.) Place the dates to cool on a sheet of waxed paper (to which they will stick slightly) or on a cake cooling rack. Eat them warm or at room temperature.

HONEY-FRIED STUFFED DATES

Stone dates, and stuff with nuts, pine-kernels, or ground pepper. Roll in salt, fry in cooked honey, and serve.

Apicius
The Roman Cookery Book, VII, xiii, 1

Rose Wine

Makes 8-10 servings

Wine-making was quite a sophisticated art in Imperial Rome, and surviving earthenware jugs often bear vintage markings. Because many wines were drunk young, however, the habit developed of adding a variety of herbs, flowers and sweeteners to soften the otherwise harsh taste.

If you have the time, desire and lots of fresh rose petals, you may like to follow Apicius' recipe to the letter. I find the use of rose water (available from most pharmacies, but make certain that it contains no glycerine) a very good match for the pace of 20th-century life.

**1 jug red or white Italian wine,
    chilled if desired
¼ cup (or more) honey
2 tablespoons (or more) rose water
Unsprayed rose petals, rinsed**

In a large decanter or punch bowl, combine the wine, honey and rose water, adjusting the flavor balance to your taste. Float rose petals on top, and serve.

ROSE WINE

Rose wine you will make like this: Thread together rose-leaves from which the white part has been removed, and steep as many as possible in wine for seven days. After seven days take the rose-leaves out of the wine, and in the same way put in other fresh rose-leaves threaded together, to rest seven days in the wine, then take them out. Repeat a third time, take out the rose-leaves, strain the wine, and, when you want to use it for drinking, add honey to make rose wine. But take care to use the best rose-leaves, when the dew has dried off them . . .

APICIUS
The Roman Cookery Book, I, iii, 1

A Medieval Christmas Feast

This borys hede we brying with song
In worchyp of hym that thus sprang
Of a virgine to redresse all wrong;
Nowell, nowelle.

From an old English Christmas carol

Since there is considerable evidence to suggest that Christ was not actually born on December 25,[1] many scholars agree that the main reason for establishing this date for the celebration of the Nativity was that the earliest Church leaders wished to substitute a Christian holiday for the well-established pagan Saturnalia. Obviously, the plan worked brilliantly.

Some centuries after the date was set, medieval England contributed a most dramatic gift to the festivities: the name itself. The word *Cristes Maesse*—literally, Mass of Christ—appears as early as 1038, and a chronicle for the year 1134 states: "This yere heald se kyng Heanri his hird [court] aet Cristes masesse on Windlesoure [Windsor]." Oddly enough, we have held on to the ancient pronunciation, for in those days *Crist* rhymed with *mist*. As time went on, we stopped pronouncing the "t" and began slurring the *mass*, arriving at the contemporary *Crissmus*, a sound which no longer vividly calls to mind the original meaning of the word.[2]

The tenacious holiday legacy of the Middle Ages is also apparent in the word *wassail*, a verbal survivor of the Anglo-Saxon *wes hál*, meaning "be in good health." By the 13th century, *wes hál* was the common salutation used when offering a cup of wine to a guest.[3]

Arthurian Christmas feasts swell the pages of medieval literature. One medieval romance begins in the midst of Christmas revelry at Camelot, where King Arthur, his Knights of the Round Table and their ladies are celebrating for 15 days, "with all the food and mirth that men knew how to devise."[4]

Merriment notwithstanding, the medieval feast was often an occasion for great pomp and ceremony. At 10 A.M. on Christmas Day, to the sound of clarion trumpets, the marshal would usher guests into the castle's great hall, seating them at long tables according to the established order of precedence.

A bowl of spiced, scented water was circulated for the hand-washing ceremony, and a Latin grace chanted in unison. Then the trumpets blared again, this time to announce the arrival of servers as they entered the hall balancing steaming platters of spit-roasted haunches, gilded fowl and enormous crusty pies.

Medieval feasts were traditionally served in three courses. Each course included a soup, followed by a wide range of baked, roasted and boiled dishes, and finally an elaborate *sotelty*, a lifelike (often edible) scene sculpted in colored marzipan or dough. One 15th-century English menu suggests bringing each of the three courses to a close with a sotelty depicting a successive phase of the Christmas story: first, the Angel Gabriel greeting Mary; second, an angel appearing before the three shepherds; third, Mary in the presence of the kings of Cologne.[5] Thus, as the feast progressed, guests participated in a dramatic, communal and gustatory celebration of the birth of Christ.

The bounty of medieval feasts is legendary. One early historian noted that in 1398, King Richard II "kept his Christmas at Liechfield, where he spent [used] in the Christmas time 200 tunns of wine, and 2000 oxen with their appurtenances."[6] A variety of choice morsels was set out to satisfy a trencherman's every whim and, at Christmas feasts, gilded peacock and festooned boar's head were highlights of the menu. Sang the servers as they presented the boar's head:

> *The boris hed in hondes I brynge,*
> *With garlondes gay and byrdes syngynge;*
> *I pray you all, helpe me to synge . . .*

Serving themselves with fingers, pointed knives and spoons—forks were not used in England until the 17th century—guests ate from trenchers, plates made of thick slabs of four-day-old bread. When thirsty, they called for the cup, and a silver goblet or bowl-shaped mazer of wine was brought to the table. Like the Prioress in Chaucer's *Canterbury Tales*, diners took care never to leave grease on the brim, for cups were shared, and slovenly table manners considered unacceptable. As one medieval etiquette book instructs:

> *Bite not thy bread and lay it down,*
> *That is no courtesy in town . . .*
> *Let never thy cheek be made too great*
> *With morsels of bread that thou shall eat . . .*
> *On both halves of thy mouth, if that thou eat,*
> *Many a skorn shall thou get . . .*
> *Nor sup not with great sounding*
> *Neither pottage nor any other thing . . .*
> *Dip not thy thumb thy drink into,*
> *Thou are uncourteous if thou it do . . . .*[7]

A Medieval Christmas Feast

Oystres in Grauey   Brede

Chawettys

Pigge Ffarced and/or Goos in Sawse Madame

Caboches in Potage

Crustade Lombard

Hippocras

Serve red or white wine with the meal and Hippocras with dessert and afterwards.

Oyster Stew

Although mussels and oysters saved many poor men from hunger during the Middle Ages, they were also valued by the rich. Numerous manuscript recipes for oyster soup call for the use of almond milk (a substitute for cow's milk made by steeping finely ground almonds in wine or water), indicating that oyster soup recipes were particularly enjoyed on some of the many fasting days, when the consumption of meat and meat products was strictly forbidden. Since more than half the days of the medieval year were considered fasting days by the Church, and since oysters were plentiful, a rich stew like this one must have been fairly standard fare.

5 cups clam juice or fish stock
1 cup white wine
½ pound blanched almonds
¼ cup chopped onions
Generous pinch each: cloves, mace, ginger, sugar
2 dozen (or more) shucked oysters

Blend the clam juice and wine in a large soup pot.

Grind the almonds to a very fine powder. (A spice grinder does the job very well.) Add the ground almonds to the liquid and stir to blend.

Submerge the onions in rapidly boiling water for 1 minute. Drain them and add them to the mixture in the pot. Heat the liquid to boiling, add the spices and simmer for a few minutes. Adjust the seasonings to taste.

Just before you are about to serve, add the oysters and cook them for about a minute. (Be sure not to overcook them as they will become rubbery.) Serve the soup in small bowls; it is quite rich and extremely delicious.

OYSTRES EN GRAUEY

◉

Take gode Mylke of Almaundys, an drawe it wyth Wyne an gode Fysshe brothe, an sette it on the fyre, & let boyle; & caste ther-to Clowes, Maces, Sugre an powder Gyngere, an a fewe parboylid Oynonys y-mynsyd. Than take fayre Oystrys, & parboyle hem in fayre Water, & caste hem there-to, an lete hem boyle to-gederys; & thanne serue hem forth.

Harleian Manuscript 279
(British Library, 15th century)

Medieval Bread

Makes 2 large round loaves

This is the only surviving bread recipe that I have been able to locate, and the instructions are tucked into a recipe for "rastons," loaves which have been hollowed out and then filled with milk-and-butter-soaked crumbs. In the Middle Ages, fermenting ale barm was used for yeast; lacking that, I use ale as the liquid ingredient and add yeast separately, with excellent results.

During the Christmas season, it was the custom of bakers to fashion little "Yulebabies" out of bread dough and give them to children for gifts. You might like to slice the loaves in half horizontally for use as trenchers (bread-plates). Don't forget to allow the trenchers to harden for four days before they are needed!

3 packages dry yeast
½ cup warm water
1½ cups ale at room temperature
2 tablespoons sugar

1 tablespoon salt
1 egg, lightly beaten
5-6 cups unbleached flour
2 tablespoons milk (optional)

BREDE

Take fayre Flowre & the whyte of Eyroun [eggs] & the yolke, a lytel. Than take Warme Berme [ale barm], & putte al thes togederys with thin hond tyl it be schort & thikke y-now, & caste Sugre y-now ther-to, & thenne lat reste a whyle. An kaste in a fayre place in the oven & late bake y-now (until done] . . . .

Harleian Manuscript 279
(British Library, 15th century)

Preheat oven to 375 degrees.

Dissolve the yeast in warm water. Combine the ale, yeast solution, sugar, salt and egg in a large bowl.

Add 4 cups of the flour and blend the ingredients by stirring with a large fork. Turn the dough onto a floured board and begin to knead it (follow the instructions for kneading in a basic cookbook; it is essential that kneading be done correctly if the bread is to have the proper texture). As you knead, work in an additional 1 to 2 cups of flour by sprinkling it on the top before folding the dough over. Stop adding flour when the dough loses its stickiness. Knead about 12 minutes, or until the dough is smooth and elastic.

Place the dough in a bowl. Cover it with a moistened cloth and set it in a warm place for 1 hour or until doubled in bulk. Punch down the dough by socking your fist into it 25 to 30 times. Divide it in 2 or 4 portions. Shape each portion into a round loaf, and place the loaves on a greased cookie sheet. Score the top twice; make about 8 diagonal slashes around the perimeter to encourage the bread to rise while baking. If you wish the top crusts to turn golden, brush them with milk.

Bake the bread for about 30 minutes. When it is done, the bread should sound hollow when you knock the top.

CHAWETTYS

*Take buttys of Vele, & mynce hem smal, or
Porke, & put on a potte; take Wyne, & caste ther-
to pouder of Gyngere, Pepir, & Safroun, & Salt, &
a lytle verthous [verjuice], & do hem in a cofyn
[pie crust] with yolkys of Eyroun [eggs], & kutte
Datys & Roysonys of Coraunce [currants], Cloyws,
Maces, & then ceuere thin cofyn, & lat it bake tyl
it be y-now [done].*

Harleian Manuscript 279
(British Library, 15th century)

Medieval Mince Pies
Makes 8 tartlets or 2 covered pies

Although lacking the suet, this recipe is ancestor apparent of the mince pie, with its combination of minced meat, spices, dates, and raisins. In the original instructions, a hint of puckering tartness was suggested by the verthous, *or verjuice, the juice of unripened grapes or crabapples. Should the latter not be available, an equivalent amount of cider vinegar may be substituted with fine results.*

During the medieval period, pie crusts were known as cofyns, or coffins, and consisted primarily of flour and water (and sometimes seasonings) molded into stiff round or rectangular shapes. These coffins were used instead of pie tins well into the 17th century, by which time special pie molds and plates were more commonly available. As a stiff coffin crust is not likely to appeal to today's palates, your choice of savory crust is recommended.

Pie pastry for 8 1¼-by-4½-inch
   tartlet shells and covers, or for
   2 9-inch shells and covers (the
   same amount of pastry is required
   in each case)
2 pounds lean veal or pork butt
   or loin
⅓ cup dry red wine
½ teaspoon ginger
Pinch saffron (optional)

½ teaspoon salt
¼ teaspoon freshly ground pepper
½ teaspoon cloves
⅛ teaspoon mace
2 teaspoons verjuice (or cider
   vinegar)
2 egg yolks (reserve whites for
   painting lids), lightly beaten
1 cup pitted, coarsely chopped dates
¼ cup currants

Preheat oven to 350 degrees.

Line the tartlet or pie shells with the pastry and place in the refrigerator until needed. Roll out the remaining pastry for the lids and refrigerate as well.

Mince the meat into tiny pieces, either by hand or in a food processor. In a large bowl, combine the minced meat with the remaining ingredients, blending them all together with your hands as you would for a meatloaf.

Divide the mixture evenly among the pastry shells. Cut out covers and set them into place. Brush the tops with the reserved egg whites and cut a few slits into the top crusts. (You may wish to use any excess pastry to create pastry cutouts and set them on the lids.)

Set the tartlets or pies on a cookie tray (to catch any drippings) and bake them for about 1 hour (slightly longer for the pies), or until the top crusts are a pale golden. You may be sure that the pork is properly cooked when the internal temperature of the mince pies registers 185 degrees on a meat thermometer.

Remove the pies from the oven and set them on a rack to cool for a few moments before serving. You may serve the tartlets in their tins or pop them out, as you wish.

Roast Suckling Pig

The Yuletide feasts of northern Europe coincided with the time known as julblot, *or the midwinter sacrifice to Frey, the god of fertility and peace. The animal most commonly sacrificed was the pig, called the* julgalt; *some folklorists believe that this ancient tradition survived through the presentation of the boar's head at Christmas feasts.*

"Pigges rosted" were served by King Richard II and the Duke of Lancaster at a feast they gave in 1387. The "pigges" were probably "endored," as it was often the custom in those days to paint roasting fowl and meat with a paste of saffron, eggs and flour to make it appear golden, a color which suggested nobility—and still does. You may wish to try endoring the roast suckling pig according to this recipe.

10-pound suckling pig, drawn, scraped and cleaned
1 tablespoon salt
7 cups breadcrumbs
2 cups (about ½ pound) grated lamb or beef kidney suet
1 tablespoon ginger
3-4 eggs, lightly beaten
Garnishes: apples, raisins, greens such as holly or parsley

FOR THE ENDORING PASTE
(Optional)

4 eggs, lightly beaten
Good pinch of saffron or safflower (an excellent, inexpensive substitute) steeped in ¼ cup hot water
Flour

PIGGE FFARCED

Take rawe egges, and drawe hem thorgh a steynour, And thene grate faire brede; And take saffrone, salt, pouder ginger, And suet of Shepe, And do medle [mix] al togidre into a faire vessell, and put hit in the pigge wombe Whane he is one [on] the brocche, And Thene sowe the hole togidre; or take a prik [skewer], and prik him togidur, And let him roste.

Harleian Manuscript 4016
(British Library, 15th century)

Preheat oven to 500 degrees.

Wash the pig well and dry both inside and out. Rub the inside with the salt.

In a large bowl, combine the breadcrumbs, suet, ginger and enough egg to make a moist filling. Place the stuffing in the cavity of the pig and sew up the hole. Place a block of wood in the pig's mouth and skewer or tie the legs into position. Cover the ears with a thick layer of cheesecloth that has been dipped in melted butter and tie the cloth into place.

Set the stuffed pig on a roasting rack in a large pan. If you wish to "endore" it, combine the eggs, saffron and enough flour to make a thickish paint. Paint about ½ of this mixture onto the pig initially; and paint it again after the first hour of baking. (The paste will thicken upon standing; you may thin it with a little water.) If you don't "endore" the pig, it is a good idea to dredge it in flour, baste it occasionally with oil or melted butter and sprinkle on additional flour.

Place the pig in a very hot oven for the first 15 minutes; then reduce the heat to 350 degrees and continue roasting for 5 to 6 hours (allow 30 minutes per pound, including stuffing), or until the internal temperature registers 185 degrees on a meat thermometer. Remove the cheesecloth from the ears for the final 15 minutes of baking.

To serve, place the pig on a very large platter. Remove the threads, skewers and wooden block. Place an apple in the pig's mouth. Set raisins into the eye sockets and weave a garland of leaves or parsley to put around the pig's neck. Surround the pig with additional greens.

NOTE: You may prepare a gravy by combining 2 tablespoons of pan drippings with 1 tablespoon of flour and, while stirring with a whisk, slowly adding 1 cup of hot stock. Season to taste with salt and pepper.

Goose in Sauce Madame

Makes 8 servings

A wide variety of fowl was eaten during the Middle Ages: chicken, capon, partridge, curlew, pigeon, quail, duck, small birds of all kinds and, of course, goose. Judging by surviving medieval menus, it would seem that most fowl was roasted whole and made golden by basting it with an egg-yolk-saffron paste. However, the recipes indicate that often fowl was cut up and served in an interesting stew such as this one. You will still have a very flavorful dish if you find it more convenient to skip the addition of the galantine.

9-pound goose
2 teaspoons coarse salt
3 cups each cored and diced pears and quinces (if quinces are out of season, replace with tart apples)
2 cups grapes, preferably seedless
15 cloves garlic, peeled

1 teaspoon dried sage
½ cup roughly chopped parsley
2 teaspoons dried hyssop
1 teaspoon dried savory
2 tablespoons galantine (see recipe below)
½ cup red wine
Optional garnish: sliced apples

SAWSE MADAME

Take sawge, parsel, ysope
[hyssop] and saueray,
quynces and peeres, garlek
and grapes, and fylle the
gees ther with and sowe
the hole that no grece
come oute and roost hem
wel, and kepe the grece
that fallith ther of. Take
galyntyne and grece and do
in a possynet [little pot].
Whan the gees buth rosted
ynowh, take & smyte hem
on pecys, and take that,
that is with inne, and do it
in a possynet and put ther
inne wyne if it be to thyk.
Do ther to powdour of
galyngale, powdour douce
[ground, sweet spice blend]
and salt, and boyle the
sawse and dresse the gees
in dishes, & lay the sewe
onoward.

The Fourme of Cury
(British Library manuscript,
Addit. 5016, c. 1390)

Preheat oven to 450 degrees.

Rub the goose inside and out with the salt.

For the stuffing, combine the fruits, garlic, sage, parsley, hyssop and savory. Stuff the cavity about three-quarters full. (Place any excess stuffing in a covered casserole and bake separately.) Sew or skewer the opening, and truss the goose in the usual way.

Roast the goose at 450 degrees for the first 15 minutes, then reduce the heat to 350 degrees and turn the goose onto its side. After 1 hour, turn the goose onto its other side. For the final 15 minutes, roast the goose on its back. Baste the goose with about 3 tablespoons of boiling water about every 20 minutes during the whole period of roasting.

(Allow about 15 minutes per pound for the total weight of the stuffed goose or approximately 2½ hours for a 9-pound stuffed goose. When the goose is done, the internal temperature should register 180 degrees, the legs should move up and down freely, and the juices—when the bird is pricked—should run a pale yellow.)

When the goose is cool enough to handle, remove the stuffing.

To prepare the sauce, combine the stuffing, galantine and wine in a large saucepan; stir to blend, and heat. Using poultry shears, remove the wings and drumsticks and carve the goose into small pieces, leaving meat on the bone whenever possible. Combine the goose pieces with the sauce; cover and rewarm a few minutes before serving. Serve on a large platter with a garnish of sliced apples around the edge.

FOR THE GALANTINE:

2 tablespoons finely ground bread
crusts
⅛ teaspoon ground galingale
Pinch each, cinnamon and ginger
2 tablespoons wine vinegar
Salt to taste

In a small bowl, combine all of the ingredients and blend until smooth.

CABOCHES IN POTAGE

Take caboches [cabbages] and quarter hem and seeth hem in gode broth with oynouns ymynced and the whyte of lekes yslyt and ycorue [carved] smale and do ther to safroun & salt and force [season] it with powdour douce [ground, sweet spice blend].

The Fourme of Cury
(British Library manuscript, Addit. 5016, c. 1390)

Cinnamon Cabbage

Makes 8 servings

It is often stated that during the Middle Ages, those who could afford to eat meat ignored vegetables. The large number of recipes for vegetables in medieval manuscript cookbooks makes such a statement seem preposterous. Although vegetables are rarely mentioned on feast menus of that time, neither are they generally listed on menus today—and we certainly consider them a necessary component of a meal.

This recipe works very nicely as a soup (if you use a cup of strong broth per person and additional spices to taste), or as a soupy vegetable prepared in the proportions that follow. It is best served on the side in individual bowls.

1 medium-size cabbage (about 2½ pounds)
2 cups chicken, beef or vegetable stock
½ teaspoon cinnamon
Scant ¼ teaspoon cloves
Pinch saffron (optional)
Salt to taste
1 medium-size onion, coarsely chopped
White of 1 large leek, coarsely chopped

Divide the cabbage into quarters and then into eighths.

In a large saucepan, bring the stock to the boil. Add the seasonings and then the cabbage, onion and leek. Cover and simmer for about 30 minutes, or until the cabbage is tender-crisp. (Turn the cabbage over after about 15 minutes of cooking.) Adjust the seasonings and serve hot.

CRUSTADE LOMBARD

Take gode creme, & leuys of Percely, & Eyroun [eggs], the yolkys & the whyte, & breke hem ther-to, & strayne thorwe a straynoure tyl it be so styf that it wol bere hym-self. Than take fayre Marwe [marrow] & Datys y-cutte in ij [2] or iij [3] & Prunes & putte the Datys an the Prunes & Marwe on a fayre Cofynne y-mad of fayre past & put the cofyn on the ovyn tyl it be a lytel hard. Thanne draw hem out of the ovyn. Take the lycour [liquid] & putte ther-on & fylle it uppe & caste Sugre y-now on, & salt; then lat it bake togederys tyl it be y-now [done]; & if it be in lente, let the Eyroun & the Marwe out & thanne serue it forth.

Harleian Manuscript 279
(British Library, 15th century)

Lombardy Custard

Makes 8 servings

This spicy fruited custard was served at King Richard II's feast given with the Duke of Lancaster on September 23, 1387. It is one of my favorite medieval dishes and always makes a hit with guests. With the combination of marrow and fruits, it seems another early variant of mincemeat.

9-inch uncooked pie pastry shell
15 each pitted prunes and dates,
  cut into small pieces
2 tablespoons raw bone marrow,
  crumbled*
3 tablespoons finely minced parsley
1 cup heavy cream
2 tablespoons brown sugar
2 eggs, lightly beaten
Pinch salt
¾ teaspoon dried orange peel
1 teaspoon cinnamon
Pinch mace

Preheat oven to 425 degrees.

Bake the pie pastry at 425 degrees for 10 minutes. Set it aside to cool.

Line the pie crust with the dried fruits. Distribute the marrow and parsley evenly over the fruit.

Combine the remaining ingredients in a bowl. (The spices are not called for in the original recipe, but make a delicious addition.) Beat until thoroughly blended. Pour the mixture over the fruits in the crust.

Bake at 375 degrees for 30 to 40 minutes, or until the custard is set and the top is brown.

Let the *crustade* cool for about 5 minutes before serving.

*Ask your butcher to hack open a beef bone so that you can easily get at the marrow.

Hippocras

These elaborate instructions for making hippocras are from a 15th-century treatise on manners and household management. If you wish a simpler method, try this recipe adapted from manuscript sources:

2 bottles burgundy wine
⅓ cup sugar
8 sticks cinnamon, broken into
   pieces
6 thin slices fresh ginger
1 teaspoon whole cloves
Pinch galingale (if available)
⅛ teaspoon freshly ground nutmeg
5 cardamom pods, coarsely crushed
¼ teaspoon grains of paradise
   (if available), finely ground

Combine the above ingredients in a large enamel pan. Bring to a boil; then reduce heat and simmer about 15 minutes, stirring occasionally. Adjust seasonings to taste. (A pleasant addition is some fresh orange or lemon peel, although these are not suggested in the original recipe.)

Strain the liquid to remove the whole spices, if you wish. Serve warm in goblets or shallow bowls.

TO MAKE HIPPOCRAS

Have three pewter basins for the liquid and three straining bags, one for each, hanging inside of them from a perch. Pare ginger or beat it into a powder and be sure to use the columbine variety. Your cinnamon sticks should be thin, brittle, and fair in color. Use grains of paradise, sugar, red wine, long pepper and turnsole for coloring. Put each spice into a separate bladder and hang these bags from the perch so that they don't touch each other. Place two or three gallons of wine into each of the basins. Allow the wine to absorb the flavors from the spice pouches. Then strain the liquid through the long cloth bag called a Hippocrate's sleeve. Taste it. If there is too much ginger, add cinnamon, and vice versa. After you have made hippocras, you can use the spice dregs in the kitchen.

Abridged and translated from JOHN RUSSELL
The Boke of Nurture (c. 1440)

A 17th-Century Christmas Banquet

Good bread and good drink, a good fire in the hall,
Brawn, pudding, and souse, and good mustard withall.
Beef, mutton, and pork, shred pies of the best,
Pig, veal, goose, and capon, and turkey well drest,
Cheese, apples, and nuts, joly carols to hear,
As then in the country, is counted good cheer.

THOMAS TUSSER
Five Hundred Points of Good Husbandry, 1557

I n the history of Christmas, no period was more tumultuous than the 17th century. The court masques (theatrical entertainments), "gaming" and dicing which had become so much a part of holiday merriment in the preceding century—Queen Elizabeth I loved to gamble—flourished in the extreme. Nicholas Breton, a writer of the period, describes the various entertainments associated with the day:

It is now Christmas, and not a cup of drink must pass without a carol; the beasts, fowl, and fish come to a general execution, and the corn [grain] is ground to dust for the bakehouse and the pastry: cards and dice purge many a purse.... Piping and dancing puts away much melancholy.... A good fire heats all the house, and a full alms-basket makes the beggar's prayers. The maskers and the mummers make the merry sport .... In sum it is a holy time, a duty in Christians for the remembrance of Christ and custom among friends for the maintenance of good fellowship.[1]

Alas, the Puritans did not agree with Breton's conclusion: "These poor, simple people," wailed Oliver Cromwell, "are mad after superstitious festivals, after unholy holidays." In 1642, ordinances were passed to suppress the performance of plays on Christmas Day, an early attempt to snap reins on holiday merrymaking. By 1647, Cromwell's Parliament came out openly against Christmas, insisting that shops remain open and that no mass be celebrated on December 25. A town crier was to be sent around the hills and dales of England proclaiming the abolition of Christmas.

For 20 years a great shadow was cast on Christmas festivities. The poet John Taylor, writing in 1646, laments:

All the liberty and harmless sports, the merry gambols, dances and friscols, with which the toiling ploughman and labourer once a year were wont to be recreated, and their spirits and hopes revived for a whole twelvement, are now extinct and put out of use . . . And to roast a sirloin of beef, to touch a collar of brawn, to bake a pie, to put a plum in the pottage pot . . . is enough to make a man to be suspected and taken for a Christian, for which he shall be apprehended for committing high Parliament Treason . . . .

Needless to say, the Parliament's attempt to abolish Christmas was a total failure. There were riots against the Puritanical edicts throughout the countryside and resolutions made that if Englishmen could not have their Christmas Day, they would put an end to Cromwell's Protectorate. Revolutionary plots were rendered unnecessary when Cromwell died in 1658 and Charles II was restored to the throne two years later. Once the "merry monarch" reigned, Father Christmas could once again be boldly heralded with holly-decked halls and songs like this one:

These holidays we'l briskly drink,
all mirth we will devise,
No Treason we will speak or think,
then bring us brave minc'd pies:
Roast Beef and brave Plum-porridge,
our Loyal hearts to chear,
Then prithee make no more ado,
but bring us Christmas Beer.

Cookbook writers lost no time in reminding readers about suitable Christmas menus, or "Bills of Fare." Robert May, in *The Accomplisht Cook* (1671), suggests 20 dishes for the first course and 19 for the second, including a dish of larks, a stuffed breast of veal, a boiled partridge, a grand "sallet," minced pies, roasted turkey "stuck with cloves," a swan pie and three brace of partridge. The bounty of the Christmas table has been legendary during most centuries, but in reality—then as now—the choice was not always quite so overwhelming. The diarist Pepys wrote on December 25, 1662: "I walked home [from Chapel] . . . with great pleasure, having there dined by my wife's bed side with great content, having a mess of brave plum-porridge and a roasted pullet for dinner, and I sent for a mince pie abroad, my wife not being well, to make any herself yet."[2]

During the 17th century, it was customary to serve meals in two main courses, each containing a variety of baked and roasted meats and "sallets," cooked and raw vegetables and greens. On special occasions, a "banquetting" course brought the meal to a dramatic close. The purpose of "banquetting conceits" was to please the eye as well as the palate, and hosts often enjoyed surprising their guests by ingenious preparations. Thus, we find recipes with instructions "To make a walnut, that when you cracke it, you shall find biskets, and carrawayes in it, or a prettie posey written,"[3] or "To make a dish of snowe" (see recipe, p. 50).

In the "dyning parlor," the table was arrayed with pewter plates, spoons, knives and, occasionally, forks.[4] Goblets of silver or Venetian glass glistened on the cupboard, and cupfuls of wine were served upon request. According to the rules of polite society, a guest never emptied the goblet, nor might he properly call for the cup more than twice during an ordinary meal. Judging by the descriptions of Christmas merrymaking, it seems reasonable to assume that this rule was relaxed on December 25.

A 17th-Century Christmas Banquet

Sowced Pigge and Mustard   Minced Pies of Mutton

Baked Stuffed Turkey

Divers Sallets Boyled

Excellent Small Cakes   A Dyschefull of Snowe

Lamb's Wool

Serve red or white wine with the meal and Lamb's Wool before or afterwards.

TO SOWCE A PIGGE

Scald a large Pigge, cut off his head and slit him in the middest, and take out his bones, and wash him in two or three warme waters. Then collar him up like Brawne, and sowe the collars in a fayre cloth. Then boyle them very tender in faire water, then take them up and throw them in fayre water and Salt untill they be colde, for that will make the skinne white. Then take a pottle of the same water, that the Pigge was boyled in, and a pottle of white Wine, a race of Ginger sliced, a couple of Nutmegs quartered, a spoonefull of whole Pepper, five or sixe Bayleaves: seeth all this together, when it is colde put your Pigge into the sowce-drincke, so you may koepe it half a yeere, but spend the head.

J. MURRELL
A New Booke of Cookerie, 1615

Soused Pork

"Sowced Pigge", or brawn, was "accounted a great piece of service at the table from November until February be ended, but chiefly in the Christmas time," noted William Harrison in his Description of England *(1577). In those days, the pickled or "sowsed" pork was generally made of domesticated boar, as the wild boar—that legendary beast of the Middle Ages—was already extinct. Pickled meats, traditionally served with mustard, were eaten in such quantity throughout the winter months that large household kitchens actually maintained a "Clark of the Sowce-tub."*

Like the boar's head, brawn (often made by pressing together the cooked and pickled meat of the boar's head itself) was usually presented at the table sporting elaborate decorations. In The Accomplisht Cook *(1687), Robert May advises: "Leach (slice) your brawn, and dish it on a plate . . . Then put a rosemary branch on the top being first dipped in the white of an egg well beaten to froth . . . or a sprig of rosemary gilt with gold." He also recommends garnishing with gilt bay leaves, carved lemons, beets and pickled grapes or gooseberries.*

Large pieces of meat were traditionally boiled in a cloth, or "collared," so that they would not disintegrate during the cooking process. As in this recipe, the collared meat was submerged in a pickling solution and thereby preserved until needed. This pickle is quite a mild one and the pork makes a good foil for some piquant mustard. Prepare this recipe a week in advance of serving.

2½-3 pounds boned loin or shoulder of pork, preferably in one piece
Cheesecloth and string for wrapping
1 bottle full-bodied white wine
10 thin slices of fresh ginger (or 1 teaspoon dried)
2 teaspoons freshly grated nutmeg
1 teaspoon whole peppercorns, bruised
2 bay leaves, scored with a knife
Garnishes: sprigs of rosemary (or holly); bay leaves; carved lemons; pickled beets; grapes; mustard (see following recipe)

Remove all but a thin layer of the fat from the pork. Wrap it in a few layers of cheesecloth and tie it securely as you would a roast. Place the "collared" pork in a large saucepan with water to cover. Bring to the boil, then reduce the heat and simmer, covered, for about 2 hours, or just until the center of the meat registers 185 degrees on a meat thermometer.

Remove the meat from the cooking liquid and submerge it in a bowl of heavily salted (about ¼ cup of salt to 2 quarts of water) cold water until it has cooled thoroughly. Reserve the cooking broth.

Meanwhile, prepare the pickling solution by combining the white wine, 3 cups of the pork broth and the spices in an enameled or stainless steel pan. Boil the liquid vigorously until it is reduced by one quarter. Set aside to cool.

Place the cooled pork in a tall glass jar. Pour in the pickling solution. Cover the jar and refrigerate for about a week, turning the pork once daily.

To serve, remove the cheesecloth and string and slice the meat. Place the slices on a serving platter, sprinkling a little of the strained marinade on top to moisten the meat. Garnish with any or all of the items mentioned above and serve with mustard on the side.

Sherry Mustard

This nutty, robust mustard is exceedingly easy to make and will last for months in a well-sealed jar in the refrigerator. Mustard was the expected accompaniment for brawn and was frequently served with beef as well. Says Grumio to Katharina in The Taming of the Shrew: *"What say you to a piece of beef and mustard?" Her reply: "A dish that I do love to feed upon." His reply: "Ay, but the mustard is too hot a little." You may find yourself in agreement.*

½ cup yellow mustard seeds
½ cup dry sherry
½ teaspoon (or more) sugar
½ teaspoon wine vinegar (optional)

Grind the mustard seeds to a coarse powder in an electric spice grinder. (This may also be done with a mortar and pestle and considerable elbow grease.) Sift out any large pieces of husk.

In a small bowl, combine the sherry, sugar and vinegar. Stir in the mustard powder with a fork. Taste and add more sugar or vinegar, if desired.

Refrigerate in a bottle with a tight-fitting lid. If the mustard gets a bit dry, simply stir in more sherry.

TO MAKE MUSTARD

. . . My Lady Holmeby makes her quick fine Mustard thus: Choose true Mustard-seed; dry it in an oven, after the bread is out. Beat and searse it to a most subtle powder. Mingle Sherry-sack with it (stirring it a long time very well) so much as to have it of a fit consistence for Mustard. Then put a good quantity of fine Sugar to it, as five or six spoonfuls, or more, to a pint of Mustard. Stir and incorporate all well together. This will keep good a long time. Some do like to put to it a little (but a little) of very sharp Wine-vinegar.

The Closet of . . .
Sir Kenelme Digbie Opened, 1669

Mincemeat Pie

Minced pies were the subject of much controversy during the 17th century. They were traditionally baked in rectangular coffins *(as pie shells were then called), a shape meant to symbolize either the crèche or Christ's sepulcher. The spices within the pie were thought to represent the gifts of the Magi. Objecting vehemently to these associations, the Puritans called the serving of minced pies on Christmas "an abomination, idolatry, superstition and popish observance," and actually outlawed them. To solve the problem, the English renamed these* coffins *"Christmas Pies," and went right along mincing the ingredients for the filling.*

1 pound very lean boneless leg of
  lamb or lamb steak, ground
½ pound beef kidney suet, ground
1 cup currants
1 cup raisins
¾ cup pitted and quartered prunes
½ teaspoon each, caraway seeds,
  ground cloves, mace, freshly
  ground nutmeg and black pepper
2 teaspoons salt
Pastry crust (see following recipe)

Preheat oven to 350 degrees.

In a large bowl, combine the ground lamb with the suet, currants, raisins, prunes, spices and salt. Blend very well with your hands. Set aside or refrigerate until needed.

Just before you are ready to bake the pie, prepare the pastry crust (see recipe). Pat the dough into the bottom and along the four sides of a 1½-quart mold or 4½-by-10-inch bread pan.

Fill the pastry with the minced meat. Place the dough lid on top and crimp the edges together. Make pastry cutouts with any left-over dough and set them on the lid. Make a hole in the center of the lid to let the steam escape. Set the pie on a baking sheet and bake for 1½ hours.

Remove the pie from the oven and let it set for 1 hour before removing it from loaf pan. (This is best done by running a knife along the edges and gently turning the pan upside down.) Spread the icing (see recipe) on top after the pie has cooled somewhat. Serve warm or at room temperature.

Pastry Crust and Icing

In the previous recipe, "to make minced Pies or Chewits of a leg of Veal . . . ," Robert May gives the following instructions: "Fill your pies, close them up, bake them, and being baked, ice them with double refined sugar, rose-water, and butter. Make the paste with a peck of flour and two pound of butter boild in fair water . . . . Make it up boiling hot . . . ."

It is important to make this crust just before you are about to line the pan, as the dough becomes stiff and brittle when cool. Do not hesitate to patch and press into place as needed; the crunchy texture of the baked dough makes the slight difficulty of rolling and shaping worthwhile.

FOR THE PASTRY CRUST:

½ pound butter
½ cup water
4 cups flour
½ teaspoon salt
2 tablespoons sugar

FOR THE ICING:

2 tablespoons butter at room temperature
5 tablespoons confectioners' sugar
½ teaspoon rose water

Combine the butter and water in a small saucepan. Bring to a boil and stir until the butter dissolves.

In a large bowl, blend the flour with the salt and sugar. Make a well in the flour mixture and slowly pour boiling liquid into the dry ingredients, stirring all the while with a fork. Knead the dough for a few moments until it is firm.

Cut off about one-third of the dough for the lid. Wrap it in a towel and set it in a warm place. Rapidly roll out the remaining dough until it is a little less than ½ inch thick. Press this dough into the baking dish. Roll out the lid as soon as the pie is filled and set it into place.

Blend the butter with confectioners' sugar and rose water in a small bowl and spread this icing as directed.

Turkey Pie

Makes 8-10 servings

Soon after the turkey was brought from the New World to Europe in the early 16th century, it gained almost immediate popularity as holiday fare, gradually replacing the swan and peacock of the medieval table. C. Anne Wilson, in Food and Drink in Britain, *claims that turkeys arrived at the London market shortly before the Christmas season, having been driven on foot for a three-month journey from as far away as Suffolk. Such well-exercised birds were likely to be tough and lean, calling for "pretty big lard" as this recipe suggests.*

Most 17th-century recipes for turkey call for roasting it "stuck with cloves." When baked in pies, the turkeys were often surrounded by clarified butter, an indication that they would be stored for use at some later date.

TO BAKE A TURKEY

Take a turkey-chicken, bone it, and lard it with pretty big lard, a pound and a half will serve, then season it with an ounce of pepper, an ounce of nutmegs, and two ounces of salt, lay some butter in the bottom of the pye, then lay on the fowl, and put in six or eight whole cloves, then put on all the seasoning with good store of butter, close it up, and baste it over with eggs, bake it, and being baked fill it up with clarified butter.

Thus you may bake them for to be eaten hot, giving them but half the seasoning, and liquor it with gravy and juyce of orange.

Bake this pye in fine paste; for more variety you may make a stuffing for it as followeth; mince some beef-suet and a little veal very fine, some sweet herbs, grated nutmeg, pepper, salt, two or three raw yolks of eggs; some boild skirrets or pieces of artichokes, grapes, or gooseberries, etc.

ROBERT MAY
The Accomplisht Cook, 1671

6-pound fresh turkey breast, boned (reserve bones)
1 teaspoon salt
½ teaspoon ground nutmeg
½ teaspoon freshly ground pepper
1 teaspoon sweet marjoram
1 teaspoon ground sage
6-8 whole cloves

FOR THE GRAVY:

1 carrot, sliced
1 onion, sliced
1 bay leaf
¼ teaspoon marjoram
¼ teaspoon ground sage
4 cups water
1 cup orange juice

FOR THE STUFFING:

½ pound ground veal
¼ pound ground beef suet
1 teaspoon sweet marjoram
1 teaspoon ground sage
¾ teaspoon salt
¼ teaspoon ground nutmeg
¼ teaspoon freshly ground pepper
8 frozen, thawed or canned artichoke hearts, cut in half
1 cup seedless grapes
⅓ cup minced parsley
2 egg yolks

FOR THE PASTRY (SEE NOTE):

6 cups flour (may be 1 cup whole wheat and 5 cups white)
1½ teaspoons salt
3 sticks (¾ pound) butter
1½ cups water

Preheat oven to 375 degrees.

First season the boned turkey breast: In a small bowl, combine the salt, nutmeg, pepper, marjoram and sage, and rub this blend on the outside and inside of the breast. Set aside.

To prepare the gravy, in a 4-quart pot, combine the turkey bones, carrot, onion, bay leaf, marjoram, sage and water and bring to a boil. Simmer for 1½ to 2 hours, skimming occasionally.

To prepare the stuffing, combine all of the ingredients in a large bowl and blend them well together with your hands. Spread the stuffing onto the inside of the turkey breast, pressing it into the crevices and openings. Fold the breast in half. Press the whole cloves, evenly spaced, into the top.

Just before you are ready to bake the turkey, make the pastry. (It is important to work rapidly with this dough as it becomes brittle and hard as it cools.) In a large bowl, mix the flour and salt. Bring the butter and water to a boil and stir until the butter melts. With a fork, stir this mixture into the flour, stirring until almost all the flour is incorporated. Knead the dough with your hands until all the flour has been absorbed. Slice off slightly more than one-third of the dough for the lid and reserve it in a warm place, wrapped in a towel. On a lightly floured board, rapidly roll out the larger portion of the dough into a rectangular shape to fit a 7-by-12-inch, 2-inch-deep Pyrex baking pan. Press the dough into the pan, patching as needed. Set the stuffed breast on the dough. Rapidly roll out the dough for the lid and place this over the breast and onto the edges of the Pyrex dish, crimping the edges with a fork. (You may also simply drape the lid over the turkey breast; make no effort to thoroughly cover the pie if the dough is not cooperating.) Use any extra dough to make pastry cutouts for decorating the lid.

Bake for 1¾ hours. Then let the turkey rest on top of the stove for about 15 minutes while you finish the gravy. Drain the bones and vegetables from the stock. (You should have about 2 cups of liquid. If not, reduce it by boiling until you have 2 cups.) Add the orange juice and bring the mixture to the boil, then simmer for 1 minute. Season to taste with salt and pepper. Transfer to a sauceboat.

To serve, carve thick slices of the turkey pie, using a serrated knife to cut through the crust (which may break, nevertheless). Spoon some of the pan juices over each slice and pass the sauceboat with additional gravy.

NOTE: As the bottom pastry becomes rather deliciously soggy with the abundant pan juices, you might prefer halving the recipe for the pastry and eliminating the bottom crust. In this case, simply butter your baking dish and proceed as above. You may also wish to eliminate the pastry altogether as the original recipe seems to suggest. In this case, you may brush the top with a mixture of 1 egg and 3 tablespoons of melted butter. In addition, you may "lard" the breast by laying about 6 slices of bacon across the top.

Gingered Spinach Salad

Makes 8 servings

According to the diarist John Evelyn, who wrote a whole book on the subject (Acetaria, A Discourse of Sallets, 1699), the composition of a salad in the 17th century was often much more complex than our salads of today. Among other things, it might "consist of Roots, Stalks, Leaves, Buds, Flowers, and Fruits." Halfway through his treatise, Evelyn gives the following advice: "Preparatory to the Dressing therefore, let your Herby Ingredients be exquisitely cull'd, and cleans'd of all worm-eaten, slimy, canker'd, dry, spotted, or any ways vitiated Leaves. And then that they be rather discreetly sprink'd, than over-much sob'd with Spring-Water, especially Lettuce . . . ."

This recipe is for a slightly cooked spinach "sallet" with an unusual butter, vinegar and spice dressing. You might wish to combine some of the additional herbs, vegetables and flowers mentioned toward the end of the original recipe to create your own version of a "boyled sallet."

3 pounds (pretrimmed weight) spinach, washed and trimmed
2 tablespoons butter
1½ tablespoons red wine vinegar
½ teaspoon cinnamon
2 teaspoons very finely minced ginger (or ½ teaspoon dried)
1 teaspoon sugar
2 tablespoons currants, plumped in boiling water, then drained
2 cups croutons
4 hard-boiled eggs, shelled and quartered

Parboil the spinach in a very large pan of boiling water for 1 minute. Drain the spinach and run cold water over it to stop the cooking process. Drain it again and squeeze it between paper towels to remove excess moisture. Finely chop the spinach.

In a large saucepan, melt the butter in the vinegar. Stir in the spices, sugar and currants. Add the spinach and stir to coat. Adjust the seasonings. (You may wish to add a pinch of salt.)

Place the croutons on a serving platter. Top with the spinach mixture and garnish with the eggs. Serve warm or at room temperature.

DIVERS SALLETS BOYLED

*Parboyle Spinage, and chop it fine, with the
edges of two hard Trenchers upon a boord, or the
backe of two chopping knives: then set them on a
Chafingdish of coales with Butter and Vinegar.
Season it with Sinamon, Ginger, Sugar, and a
few parboyld Currins. Then cut hard Egges into
quarters to garnish it withall, and serve it upon
sippets. So may you serue Burrage, Buglosse,
Endiffe, Suckory, Coleflowers, Sorrel, Marigold
leaves, water-Cresses, Leekes boyled, Onions,
Sparragus, Rocket, Alexanders. Parboyle them,
and season them all alike: whether it be with
Oyle and Vinegar, or Butter and Vinegar,
Sinamon, Ginger, Sugar, and Butter: Egges are
necessary, or at least very good for all boyld
Sallets.*

J. MURRELL
A New Booke of Cookerie, 1615

EXCELLENT SMALL CAKES

Take three pound of very fine flower well dryed by the fire, and put to it a pound and half of loaf Sugar sifted in a very fine sieve and dryed; Three pounds of Currants well washed and dryed in a cloth and set by the fire; When your flower is well mixed with the Sugar and Currants, you must put in it a pound and half of unmelted butter, ten spoonfuls of Cream, with the yolks of three new-laid Eggs beat with it, one Nutmeg; and if you please, three spoonfuls of Sack. When you have wrought your paste well, you must put it in a cloth, and set it in a dish before the fire till it be through warm. Then make them up in little Cakes, and prick them full of holes; you must bake them in a quick oven unclosed. Afterwards Ice them over with Sugar. The Cakes should be about the bigness of a hand-breadth and thin: of the cise of the Sugar Cakes sold at Barnet.

The Closet of . . .
Sir Kenelme Digbie Opened, 1669

Currant Butter Cookies   *Makes 2½ dozen cookies or 2-inch "cakes"*

The term "cake" was often used during this period for the sweet and spicy baked goods we now call cookies. This recipe, with its outrageous proportion of currants to dough, is one of the best secrets Sir Kenelme Digbie revealed when he opened his closet (private chamber) and wrote his cookbook.

1¾ cups flour
1 cup sugar
2 cups currants
2 tablespoons cream
1 egg yolk
½ teaspoon ground nutmeg
1 tablespoon sherry
¼ pound butter, melted

Preheat oven to 375 degrees.

Lightly butter 2 cookie sheets and set them aside. In a large bowl, mix the flour, sugar and currants. In another bowl, stir the cream, yolk, nutmeg and sherry together.

Stir the melted butter and the cream mixture into the flour mixture with a fork. Then knead the dough briefly with your hands.

To shape the cookies, pat about 2 tablespoons of dough between your hands to form 2-inch oval discs about ¼ inch thick. Place them on the lightly greased cookie sheets. (The dough may seem awkward to shape because it contains so many currants. Don't get discouraged, and try not to let any currants slip away.)

Bake the cookies for 15 minutes and transfer them to a rack to cool. Store them in an airtight container.

To Make Snow

This lovely and delicious "dish of snowe" is a delightful "banquetting conceit" for drawing your holiday meal to a close.

1 cup heavy cream
2 tablespoons confectioners' sugar
1 tablespoon (or more) rose water
1 egg white
1 large apple
1 generous sprig of fresh rosemary
   or evergreen
1 dozen wafers, plain butter cookies,
   or "excellent small cakes" (see
   preceding recipe)

In a medium-sized bowl, whip the cream and sugar until stiff. Stir in the rose water. Taste and add more rose water, if desired.

In a small bowl, beat the egg white until it forms stiff peaks. Fold the egg white into the whipped cream.

Place the apple in the center of a small chilled platter. Press the rosemary into the core of the apple. Splash some "snow" onto the rosemary and the remainder around the apple. Set the cookies as a border around the cream. To serve, let guests choose the cookies and offer the "snow" for a topping or dip.

A DYSCHEFULL OF SNOWE

At Christmas I no more desire
   a Rose
Than wish a Snow in Mayes
   new-fangled showes,
But like of each thing
        that in season grows.

WILLIAM SHAKESPEARE
Love's Labour's Lost, 1588

To make a Dyschefull of Snowe Take a pottell [half gallon] of swete thycke creame and the whytes of eyghte egges, and beate them altogether wyth a spone. Then putte them in youre creme and a saucerfull of Rosewater, and a dyshe full of Suger wyth all. Then take a stycke and make it cleane, and than cutte it in the ende foure square, and therwith beate all the aforesayde thynges together, and ever as it ryseth take it of and put it into a Collaunder. This done, take one apple and set it in the myddes of it, and a thicke bushe of Rosemary, and set it in the myddes of the platter. Then cast your Snowe uppon the Rosemarye and fyll your platter therwith. And yf you have wafers caste some in wyth all and thus serve them forthe.

A Proper Newe Booke of Cokerye
(Cambridge manuscript, c. 1560)[5]

LAMB'S WOOL

Next crowne the bowle full
With gentle lamb's wooll;
Adde sugar, nutmeg and ginger;
With store of ale too;
And thus ye must doe
To make the Wassaile a swinger.

ROBERT HERRICK (1591-1674)

Lamb's Wool: A Wassail Bowl

Makes 8 4-ounce servings

This traditional holiday drink—a kind of wassail bowl—derives its name from the pulp of roasted apples floating on the top. Usually they were crab apples: Shakespeare has described winter as a time "when roasted crabs hiss in the bowl."

The word wassail, from the Old English wes hål, *literally means to "be in good health." It was often the custom to float toasted bread on top of the steaming, spiced liquid, hence the presumed origin of our expression "to propose a toast."*

Modern-day wassail recipes usually call for a combination of sherry and brandy plus sugar, spices and eggs. The following recipe is dramatically different (evidence of just how much a recipe can change over the years) and may not be to everyone's taste, so modest servings are suggested.

1½ pounds apples, cored
1 quart ale
1 tablespoon (or more) sugar
⅛ teaspoon each, ground ginger
and freshly ground nutmeg

Preheat oven to 375 degrees.

Bake the apples in a large dish for about 45 minutes, or until they burst. Set them aside to cool.

When the apples are cool enough to handle, remove the peel and mash the pulp. You should have about 1½ cups.

In a large pot, heat the ale. With a whisk, blend in the apple pulp, sugar and spices. Adjust the seasonings to taste.

Place the mixture in a festive bowl and sprinkle the top with some additional freshly grated nutmeg. Serve hot in small mugs.

Christmas in the Pudding Age

Now enter Christmas like a man,
Armed with spit and dripping-pan,
Attended with pasty, plum-pie,
Puddings, plum-porridge, furmity . . .
Pig, swan, goose, rabbits, partridge, teal,
With legs and loins and breasts of veal,
But above all the minced pies
Must mentioned be in any wise . . . .

from Poor Robin's Almanack, 1701

The 18th century was known as the Pudding Age, when the expression "to come in pudding-time" meant to arrive at a lucky moment. During the Pudding Age, Christmas cookery was done in a big way—literally. There are records of one particular pudding made for an Exeter fair which contained 400 pounds of flour, 170 pounds of beef suet, 140 pounds of raisins and 240 eggs. The pudding weighed in at about 800 pounds and required continuous boiling for four days. When finally done, it was drawn through the streets on a cart pulled by eight oxen, then cut up and distributed to the poor.[1]

Hannah Glasse, in her famous *The Art of Cookery Made Plain and Easy* (1747), gives the following extraordinary recipe for "A Yorkshire Christmas-Pye." She claims that they "are often sent to London in a Box as Presents; therefore the walls must be well built":

First make a good Standing Crust, let the Wall and
Bottom be very thick, bone a Turkey, a Goose, a Fowl, a
Partridge, and a Pigeon, season them all very well, take
half an Ounce of Mace, half an Ounce of Nutmegs, a
quarter of an Ounce of Cloves, and half an Ounce of
black Pepper, all beat fine together, two large Spoonfuls
of Salt, mix them together. Open the Fowls all down the
Back, and bone them . . . Season them all well first, and
lay them in the crust . . . Then have a Hare ready cased,
and wiped with a clean Cloth . . . Cut it to Pieces . . .;

season it, and lay it as close as you can on one Side; on
the other Side Woodcock, more Game, and what Sort of
wild Fowl you can get. Season them well, and lay them
close; put at least four Pounds of Butter into the Pye,
then lay on your Lid, which must be a very thick one,
and let it be well baked. It must have a very hot Oven,
and will take at least four Hours . . . .

It had been the practice during previous centuries for the wealthy to open their homes to the poor on Christmas Day, and there was some concern during the 18th century that this custom would be forgotten. The fictitious Sir Roger de Coverley, a recurrent character in the *Spectator,* a popular newspaper of the time, was presented as the ideal country gentleman when he always kept his open house at Christmas: "He had killed eight fat hogs for this season . . . had dealt about his chines very liberally amongst his neighbours, and . . . had sent a string of hog's puddings [sausages] with a pack of cards to every poor family in the parish."

"I have often thought," Sir Roger is quoted as saying, "it happens well that Christmas should fall out in the middle of winter. It is the most dead uncomfortable time of the year, when the poor people would suffer very much from their poverty and cold, if they had not good cheer, warm fires, and Christmas gambols to support them."[2]

During much of the 18th century, there was a great regard for order and symmetry, esthetic goals that were as much in evidence on dining tables as in formal gardens. According to the custom of the age, each dinner guest was provided a "cover" consisting of a dinner plate of silver or porcelain, a fork, knife, spoon, napkin and wineglass. Many cookbooks of the period present elaborate diagrams of table settings and the proper placement of serving platters. The lady of the house did the "Honours of the Table" from her position at the head. For the first course, she served the soup from a large tureen into individual bowls which were passed along to the guests by servants. As soon as she was done, the tureen was removed and a large roast immediately put in its place. It was then the lady's task to do the carving, her husband carrying on the same task with another roast at the opposite end of the table.

The meal generally consisted of soup plus two main courses, or "removes," followed by an elaborate display of desserts: ice cream, whipped syllabubs, biscuits, and sweetmeats of all kinds. After the meal, the men remained behind to drink toasts with wine and brandy while the ladies retired to the drawing room.

One gentleman's Christmas dinner was so elaborate, he claims: "'Tis impossible for me to give you half our bill of fare, so you must be content to know that we had turkies, geese, capons, puddings of a dozen sorts more than I had ever seen in my life, besides brawn, roast beef, and many things of which I know not the names, minc'd pyes in abundance, and a thing they call plumb pottage . . . . Our wines were of the best, as were all the rest of our liquors . . . . If a stranger were to have made an estimate of London from this place, he would imagine it not only the richest but the most happy city in the world."[3]

Christmas in the Pudding Age

Plum-Porridge
Salmagundy
Sirloin of Beef* and Yorkshire Pudding   Stuffed Shoulder of Mutton
Artichoke Puding
A Plum Puding Baked   Ginger Bread
Brandy Posset

Serve the wine of your choice during the meal and brandy afterwards.

*As standard recipes for roast beef are readily available, no recipe is given.

Plum Porridge

Recipes for plum porridge date back at least to the Elizabethan period. By the late 17th century, the fruited broth had become linked to Christmas and was often referred to as Christmas pottage or, when thickened with breadcrumbs or sago, Christmas porridge. The preservative effect of the sugar and other sweet ingredients suggested in this original recipe made it possible for the cook to prepare the soup in advance and store it in earthen containers until needed.

This is a fascinating soup with many levels of flavor, a characteristic not unusual for plum porridge. According to a Mr. Thomas North writing to Read's Weekly Journal *on January 9, 1731, the plum pottage he recently enjoyed seemed "to have 50 different tastes." It is wise to serve small portions, though, as this plum porridge is both rich and sweet.*

**2 pounds shin of beef on the bone,
  hacked into 2-inch pieces**
**2 cups fresh or dry white bread,
  crumbled**
1 cup currants
1 cup raisins
⅓ cup pitted prunes, halved
¼ teaspoon each, mace and nutmeg
⅛ teaspoon ground cloves
¼ cup (or less) sugar
½ teaspoon salt
¼ cup dry sherry
¼ cup red wine
1 tablespoon (or more) lemon juice

PLUM-PORRIDGE FOR CHRISTMAS

Take a Leg and Shin of Beef, put to them eight Gallons of Water, and boil them till they are very tender; and when the Broth is strong, strain it out; wipe the Pot and put in the Broth again; then slice six Penny-loaves thin, cut off the Top and Bottom, put some of the Liquor to it, cover it up, and let it stand a Quarter of an Hour, boil it and strain it, and then put it into your Pot; let it boil a Quarter of an Hour, then put in five Pounds of Currants, clean washed and picked; let them boil a little, and put in five Pounds of Raisins of the Sun stoned, and two Pound of Pruens, and let them boil till they swell; then put in three Quarters of an Ounce of Mace, half an Ounce of Cloves, two Nutmegs, all of them beat fine, and mix it with a little Liquor cold, and put them in a very little while, and take off the Pot, then put in three Pounds of Sugar, a little Salt, a Quart of Sack, a Quart of Claret, the Juice of two or three Lemons. You may thicken with Sego instead of Bread, if you please; pour them into earthen Pans, and keep them for Use . . . .

HANNAH GLASSE
The Art of Cookery Made Plain and Easy, 1747

In a large soup pot, bring the shin of beef with 3 quarts of water to a boil. Simmer gently for 4 hours, skimming the foam off the top as needed. Strain the liquid through a cheesecloth-lined sieve and reserve the broth.

In a small saucepan, combine 2 cups of this broth with the bread. Simmer for 10 minutes, stirring frequently to prevent the bottom from burning. Strain the bread mixture through a sieve or puree it in a food processor. Return the mixture to the remaining broth and simmer the liquid for 15 minutes. Stir every now and then to prevent scorching.

Add the currants and simmer for 5 minutes. Add the raisins and prunes and simmer for an additional 5 minutes. Add the spices, sugar and salt and simmer for 1 minute, or until the sugar is dissolved. Remove the pot from the heat and add the sherry, wine and lemon juice. Adjust the seasonings and serve hot.

Salmagundy

"His mind was a sort of salmagundy," claimed one prose writer of the period, making an analogy to the kaleidoscope of ingredients in this cold salad platter. The goal of a salmagundy was to set forth a visually attractive array, being careful to establish a nice balance between the pickled or salted foods and the bland ones. A version similar to this appears in the first edition (1747) of Mrs. Glasse's very popular cookbook.

6-8 pickled herring fillets, minced
2 large apples, cored, peeled and
    sliced
1 onion, peeled and chopped
2 hard-boiled eggs (finely chop the
    yolks and whites separately)
1 cup sliced gherkins
1 cup diced celery
1 pound pickled red cabbage
    (or sauerkraut)
Garnishes: watercress, nasturtiums
    (or other edible, unsprayed flower
    petals)

FOR THE DRESSING:

¾ cup salad oil
¼ cup wine vinegar
2 tablespoons lemon juice
Salt to taste

Set out the above ingredients in small bowls and arrange them on a large tray or platter. Garnish with sprigs of watercress and flower petals, if available.

For the dressing, in a small jar combine the ingredients and shake them together well. Pour the dressing into a pitcher or sauceboat and serve it on the side.

Yorkshire Pudding

Makes 8 servings

*In the 18th century, the "Roast Beef of Old England" came to the height of its glory, having been
knighted (so the legend goes) as Sir Loin by Charles II in one of his merry moods. In its grandest hour,
the "Baron of Beef" was served like a saddle of mutton, that is, the two loins remained attached by the
backbone. The traditional garnish was horseradish.*

*In the view of Peter Kalm, a Swedish traveler of the period, "The Englishmen understand almost bet-
ter than any other people the art of properly roasting a joint . . . [it] has a fatness and a delicious taste,
either because of the excellent pasture . . . or some way of fattening the cattle known to the butchers
alone." One day, a cook was inspired to create a clever, superb and economical dish by placing batter in
the dripping pan that sat below every roasting joint to catch the fats and juices. The result: Yorkshire
pudding.*

*Recipes for Yorkshire pudding vary, from the thick and stodgy to the light and custardy. This recipe
finds a delicate balance between the two. You may bake it in a separate pan, or you may pour the batter
directly into the roasting pan (that is, if your roast is set on a rack and almost done), but in this case
check after 15 minutes, as the pudding is likely to puff up very quickly.*

2 tablespoons butter or pan
   drippings
2 eggs
2 cups milk
⅛ teaspoon salt
1¼ cups flour

Preheat oven to 400 degrees.

Place the butter or drippings in a large, rectangular baking pan, such as a 7½-by-11¾-inch Pyrex dish. Set the pan in the oven so that the fat will melt while you make the batter.

In a large bowl, combine the eggs and milk using an electric beater. Add the salt and gradually add the flour, beating all the while. Beat a total of about 5 minutes altogether.

Pour the batter into the heated pan and bake for about 20 minutes, or until the custard is set and the top is pale yellow and the sides a golden brown.

NOTE: Prepared with butter, Yorkshire Pudding is delicious as a breakfast pancake served with jam.

A YORKSHIRE PUDDING

Take a Quart of Milk, four Eggs, and a little Salt, make it up into a thick Batter with Flour, like a Pancake Batter. You must have a good Piece of Meat at the Fire, take a Stew-pan and put some Dripping in, set it on the Fire; when it boils, pour in your Pudding; let it bake on the Fire till you think it is nigh enough, then turn a Plate upside-down in the Dripping-pan, that the Dripping may not be blacked; set your Stew-pan on it under your Meat, and let the Dripping drop on the Pudding, and the Heat of the Fire come to it, to make it of a fine brown. When your Meat is done and set [sic] to Table, drain all the Fat from your Pudding, and set it on the Fire again to dry a little; then slide it as dry as you can into a Dish, melt some Butter, and pour into a Cup, and set in the Middle of the Pudding. It is an exceeding good Pudding; the Gravy of the Meat eats well with it.

HANNAH GLASSE
The Art of Cookery Made Plain and Easy, 1747

Leg of Lamb Stuffed with Oysters

Makes 8 servings

The combination of lamb and oysters is typical of the 18th century, a time when oysters were cheap and plentiful. The flavors work beautifully together and this stuffed leg of lamb, when sliced, makes a very attractive presentation.

8-pound leg of lamb (see instructions for butcher below)

FOR THE STUFFING:

2 tablespoons grated beef suet
1 cup breadcrumbs
2 hard-boiled egg yolks, chopped
6 anchovy fillets, drained and chopped
¼ cup chopped onion
⅛ teaspoon salt (optional)
⅛ teaspoon each, freshly ground pepper and nutmeg
½ teaspoon each, dried thyme and winter savory
1 dozen shucked oysters in their own juice
1 large egg, lightly beaten

FOR THE SAUCE:

¼ cup (approximately) oyster liquid or bottled clam juice
1 cup red wine
4 anchovy fillets, finely chopped
Pinch freshly ground nutmeg
½ small onion, peeled

TO STUFF A SHOULDER OR LEG OF MUTTON WITH OYSTERS

Take a little grated bread, some beef-suet, yolks of hard eggs, three anchovies, a bit of an onion, salt, pepper, thyme, winter-savoury, twelve oysters, and some nutmeg grated: Mix all these together, shred them very fine, and work them up with raw eggs, like a paste; stuff your mutton under the skin in the thickest place, or where you please, and roast it; for sauce take some of the oyster liquor, some claret, two or three anchovies, a little nutmeg, a bit of onion, and the rest of the oysters: stew all these together, then take out the onion, and put it under the mutton.

E. SMITH
The Compleat Housewife, 1753

Preheat oven to 450 degrees.

Ask your butcher to remove the skin and fell from the leg of lamb, and then to remove the bone itself, leaving an enclosed pocket for the stuffing. (He might also remove the small gland from the leg as it has a rather strong taste.) You should be left with about 5 pounds of meat. Bring the meat to room temperature before you begin to cook it.

To prepare the stuffing, combine the ingredients (using only 7 of the oysters and reserving the liquid for the sauce) into a paste in the food processor or blender. Place as much of this stuffing as will comfortably fit into the pocket of the leg of lamb. Sew and/or bind the pocket closed with string.

Place the stuffed leg of lamb on a roasting rack in a large roasting pan. Set the lamb in the oven and immediately reduce the temperature to 350 degrees. Bake for about 2½ hours or until the internal temperature in the center registers 160 degrees (for pink lamb) or 175 degrees (for well done) on a meat thermometer. When done, let the lamb sit at room temperature for about 10 minutes before removing the string and slicing the meat.

To prepare the sauce, combine the ingredients (except the oysters) in a small saucepan and simmer for about 15 minutes, stirring occasionally. (You may enrich the sauce by pouring out the fat from the roasting pan, deglazing the pan with additional wine, and adding this liquid to the simmering mixture.) Just before you are ready to serve, remove the onion, dice the oysters, and add them for a final 30 seconds. Remove to a sauceboat and serve with the lamb.

Artichoke Pudding

Makes 6-8 servings

"The Pudding is a Dish very difficult to be describ'd, because of the several Sorts there are of it . . . " explained the French traveler Misson, upon his return from a trip to England. "They bake them in an Oven, they boil them with Meat, they make them fifty several Ways. BLESSED BE HE THAT INVENTED PUDDING!"

I hope that Misson had the opportunity to taste artichoke pudding; it is a beguiling dish which belies the general conception of puddings as indelicate and stodgy.

FOR THE PUDDING:

2 packages frozen artichoke hearts
3 large eggs plus 3 yolks, well beaten
2 cups heavy cream
1½ teaspoons salt
2 teaspoons rose water
1 teaspoon (or more) sugar

FOR THE SAUCE:

½ cup sherry
2 tablespoons butter, cut into bits
Sugar

Preheat oven to 375 degrees.

Boil the artichoke hearts in salted water to cover until they are soft. In a blender, puree the artichoke hearts. Pass the puree through a fine-meshed strainer into a bowl. Set aside.

In a large bowl, combine the eggs, cream, salt, rose water and sugar. Beat until foamy. Fold the egg mixture into the artichoke puree and pour into a buttered 1½-quart soufflé dish or casserole.

Bake at 375 degrees for 30 minutes, or until the pudding is set. To prepare the sauce, in a saucepan, heat the sherry. Whisk in the butter and sugar to taste. Pour the sauce over the pudding, or serve it on the side in a sauceboat.

AN ARTICHOKE PUDIN[G]

*Take 8 artichoks boyle ym [them] tell ye [they] be
tender yn [then] take of all ye leves of & core &
strings out yn beat ym well in a bole & forse ym
through a hare sive yn have redy 6 eggs lave out 3
whits beat ym yn beat ym with ye artichoks very
well yn mix ym with a pint of crame a litle salt
rose water & sugar too yr [your] tast buter yr pan
well halfe an oure will bake it sarve it with sack or
white wine buter & suger.*

PENELOPE PEMBERTON
Manuscript Cookery Book
(Szathmary Archives, 18th century)

Baked Plum Pudding

Makes 8-10 servings

This is a wonderful, fruit-packed, old-fashioned bread pudding. However, you may wonder that there are no plums (or prunes) in it, despite the name. The curious fact that most English plum puddings contain no plums has been explained by the claim that the dried plums imported by the Elizabethans were held in such esteem that the word plum came to be used in reference to other dried fruits (especially raisins and currants) even when plums were not used or available.

**15 thin slices white bread, crusts
  removed**
1 quart milk
1 teaspoon freshly grated nutmeg
Pinch salt
4 large eggs
1 cup (¼ pound) grated suet
2 cups (loosely packed) currants
**1½ cups (loosely packed) raisins
  (I like to use yellow raisins for
  flavor and color contrast)**

Preheat oven to 350 degrees.

At least 6 hours or the night before you intend to bake the pudding, layer the bread in a large pan. Bring the milk to the boil, stir in the nutmeg and salt, and pour the milk evenly over the bread. Cover with waxed paper and set aside until a few hours before you are ready to eat the pudding.

Place the bread-milk mixture into a large bowl. Beat the mixture with an electric beater, adding 1 egg at a time as you continue to beat. When all the eggs are well blended in, add the suet and continue beating. Finally, stir in the currants and raisins.

Pour the mixture into a large, buttered, shallow pan (such as a 7½-by-11¾-inch Pyrex baking dish) and bake for 40 minutes, or until the custard is set. Serve warm.

A PLUM PUDING BAKED:
MY AUNT FFRANCKLINES RECEIPT

Take a peny lofe (but of London bread take a little more) cutt of the crust, and slice the crume very thine, then boyle a quart of milke and put it boyleing hott to the bread, and grate some nuttmeg to it, so let it stand all night, and the next morning put foure eggs into it, and beat them very well in the bread, and milke, and as you beat it strew in a little flower, till you have made it of a fitt thickness, it must not be too thine for then all the plums will sink to the bottome, neither must you make it too thike for then it will not be so light, you must keep it with continuall beating for a great while, for that will make it light, then put in about a quarter of a pounde of suet cutt very small, stir it in well, then wash almost halfe a pounde of courence, and as many raisons, and shake them very well in a cloath till they are drye, and stir them well in the puding, with a little salt, and so bake it in a puter dish, well buttered.

REBECCA PRICE
The Compleat Cook, compiled 1681-1740

GINGER BREAD

Take 3 quarters of a pound of sugar, an ounce and half of Ginger, half an ounce of Cinamon in fine pouder. Mingle all these with your flower, and make it up with 3 pound of Treacle, just so stif as well keep it from running about ye board; then put in 3 quarters of a pound of Melted butter, and stirring it well togeather; then strow in some more flower by degrees, enough to make it so stif as will make it up in cakes. The Oven must be no hotter than for manchets [white loaves], lett it stand in ye Oven 3 quarters of an hour; wash out the treacle with 2 or 3 spoonsfull of Milk, bake it on butter'd papers; mince in also 2 ounces of Oringe pill, and preserved sittern [citron] 2 ounces, and 2 great nuttmegs grated.

The Receipt Book of Ann Blencowe, 1694

Gingerbread

Makes 16 3-inch cookies or gingerbread men

Gingerbread has had an interesting evolution. In the medieval and Tudor periods it was made by blending breadcrumbs into honey and adding spices such as ginger, cinnamon, cloves and licorice—sometimes even pepper. The mixture was boiled, shaped into loaves and sometimes stamped with decorative designs.

With the increased production of refined sugar in the late 17th century came the by-product molasses, known as treacle in England. Gradually molasses replaced honey as the primary sweetener, but judging by the number of recipes in early cookbooks, gingerbread remained as popular as ever.

½ cup sugar
2 tablespoons ginger
1½ teaspoons cinnamon
2 teaspoons freshly grated nutmeg
3½-4 cups flour
1½ cups molasses
1 tablespoon milk
¼ pound melted butter, cooled

2 tablespoons coarsely chopped citron
2 tablespoons coarsely chopped candied orange peel
Optional garnishes: currants or chopped blanched almonds

Preheat oven to 375 degrees.

Line 2 cookie sheets with baking parchment, or grease and flour them well. Set aside.

Sift the sugar, ginger, cinnamon and nutmeg with 1½ cups of the flour. Add the molasses, milk, melted butter, citron and orange peel. Stir vigorously with a wooden spoon. Gradually work in the remaining flour until it is well absorbed and you have a very thick, but slightly sticky batter.

With well-floured hands, break off pieces of dough about ¼ cup each. Shape the dough into circles, rectangles or rough little gingerbread men about ½ inch thick. (You will need to work fairly quickly and flour your hands each time you pick up more dough.) Make decorative marks on the cakes with a sharp knife and use currants or nuts to mark the eyes, nose and mouth.

Bake for 20 minutes, or just until edges begin to darken slightly. Cool on a rack; the gingerbread will become considerably harder as it cools. Store in an airtight container until needed.

NOTE: You may also wish to shape the dough into 2 very large gingerbread men.

TO MAKE A BRANDY POSSET

Boil a quart of cream over a slow fire, with a stick of cinnamon in it, take it off to cool, beat the yolks of six eggs very well, and mix them with the cream, add nutmeg and sugar to your taste, set it over a slow fire, and stir it one way; when it is like a fine thin custard, take it off, and pour it into your turene or bowl, with a glass of brandy, stir it gently together, and serve it up with tea wafers round it.

ELIZABETH RAFFALD
The Experienced English-Housekeeper, 1782

Brandy Posset

Possets are smooth, soothing drinks, so rich that they are almost a meal in themselves—and the ideal way to warm up after an evening of caroling.

1 **quart heavy cream**
1 **stick cinnamon, broken in two**
6 **egg yolks, lightly beaten**
⅛ **teaspoon (or more) freshly grated nutmeg**
2 **tablespoons sugar**
½ **cup brandy**
Wafers or butter cookies

In a heavy-bottomed pot, boil the cream with the cinnamon stick for a few minutes over medium heat. Remove the pot from the heat and whisk the cream vigorously to cool it slightly. Gradually whisk in the egg yolks and add the nutmeg and sugar. Simmer the mixture over low heat, stirring constantly, until it thickens slightly. (Take care not to boil it because the yolks will curdle.) Add the brandy and pour the mixture into a small bowl or into individual mugs. Sprinkle some additional nutmeg or cinnamon on top, if desired, and serve with cookies or wafers.

A Victorian Christmas Dinner

Christmas is coming, the geese are getting fat,
Please to put a penny in the old man's hat;
If you haven't got a penny, a ha'penny will do,
If you haven't got a ha'penny, God bless you!

An old beggar's rhyme

Mention the words "Victorian Christmas Dinner" and what scene jumps to mind but the hungry Cratchit family poised to begin their eagerly anticipated repast. As Dickens relates in *A Christmas Carol:*

At last the dishes were set on, and grace was said. It was succeeded by a breathless pause, as Mrs. Cratchit, looking slowly all along the carving-knife, prepared to plunge it in the breast.... Bob said he didn't believe there ever was such a goose cooked. Its tenderness and flavour, size and cheapness, were the themes of universal admiration. Eked out by apple-sauce and mashed potatoes, it was a sufficient dinner for the whole family .... Every one had had enough, and the youngest Cratchits in particular were steeped in sage and onion to the eyebrows ....

It was during the Victorian period that Christmas came to be the holiday that we celebrate today. Only in the 19th century did the Christmas tree become an essential part of the festivities, though the idea of decorating an evergreen for winter festivals can be traced back to pagan times. The most immediate impetus for doing this at Christmas came from Germany, where it had become fashionable in many homes to have a tree whose "boughs bent under the weight of gilt oranges, almonds, etc., and under it was a neat model of a farm house, surrounded by figures of animals, etc., and all due accompaniments."[1] In 1840, Queen Victoria and her new husband, the German Prince Albert, had a Christmas tree, and once it had that royal imprimatur, Christmas evergreens spread their boughs in homes throughout the country. Sadly, the Victorian habit of decorating the tree with sweetmeats and fruits (eaten by the children on Twelfth Night) has given way in most homes to ornaments of the inedible variety.

It was also the Victorians who exchanged the first Christmas cards. There is much controversy about who originated the idea, but by mid-century, hand-wrought cards were common, and 25 years later, printed cards were being produced by the thousands in all shapes and sizes: Christmas bells, scrolls, stars and fans were made of silk and satin with the sender's name and greetings embossed in gold.

Counterbalancing the increasing commercialization of Christmas were the many old, enduring country traditions. One such was called "wassailing the apple trees" on Christmas Eve. Although custom varied from region to region, the underlying belief shared by all who participated was that drinking toasts to the trees in the orchard assured bountiful future harvests. Spirited wassailers chanted lines like the following to increase their merriment:

> *Apples and pears, with right good corn*
> *Come in plenty to every one;*
> *Eat and drink good cake and hot ale,*
> *Give earth to drink, and she'll not fail.*[2]

Another strongly abiding folk custom was "Bringing in the Yule Log" to insure good luck for the coming year. All agreed that the log had to be lit with a brand from last year's; in some households, the log had to be large enough to burn (or at least smolder) on the hearth for the full 12 days of Christmas—the loss of firelight being thought equivalent to the loss of good luck. To everyone, the Yule log was a symbol of the warm welcome given to all during the Christmas season and watching it burn provided much occasion for holiday cheer.

The elegant Victorian dinner table would be likely to appear to us as a kaleidoscope of special effects, with utensils provided for every imaginable purpose. In addition to the ordinary basic table setting, most diners were outfitted with asparagus tongs, oyster forks, marrow spoons and fruit knives, not to mention the spoon warmers, butter coolers and knife rests. With dessert, that newfangled invention the "finger glass" would make its appearance. Instructs one etiquette specialist of the period:

> *Finger glasses, filled with warm water, come on with the dessert. Wet a corner of your napkin, and wipe your mouth, then rinse your fingers; but do not practise the filthy custom of gargling your mouth at table, albeit the usage prevails amongst a few, who think, because it is a foreign habit, it cannot be disgusting.*[3]

Mrs. Beeton, in her voluminous *Book of Household Management* (1861), suggests a December dinner for 12. She recommends a first course of soup and fish; entrées of beef filets, fricasseed chicken, oyster patties and curried rabbit; a second course of roast turkey, boiled leg of pork, roast goose and stewed beef; a third course of widgeon, partridges, *charlotte aux pommes*, mince pies, orange jelly, lemon cream, apple tart and cabinet pudding. To follow all of that: dessert and ices.

Here is a more modest Bill of Fare for a Christmas dinner, sumptuous nevertheless.

A
Victorian
Christmas Dinner

Oyster Loaves

Roast Stuffed Goose [and vegetables of your choosing]

Superlative Mincemeat   Mince Pies Royal

Christmas Pudding with Punch Sauce

Shrub

Serve the wine of your choice during the meal and shrub before or afterwards.

Individual Oyster Loaves

Makes 8 servings

The oyster has always been an abundantly popular English food, among rich and poor alike. Mrs. Beeton explains that "The oyster fishery in Britain is esteemed of so much importance, that it is regulated by a Court of Admiralty. In the month of May, the fishermen are allowed to take the oysters, in order to separate the spawn from the cultch, the latter of which is thrown in again, to preserve the bed for the future. After this month, it is felony to carry away the cultch, and otherwise punishable to take any oyster, between the shells of which, when closed, a shilling will rattle." Clearly, by Victorian times, the seemingly inexhaustible supply of oysters was dwindling fast.

8 brioches or dinner rolls (about
   4 inches in diameter)
2 dozen large (or more, if small)
   shucked oysters in their own
   juice
2 tablespoons sweet butter
2 teaspoons flour
6 tablespoons heavy cream
Freshly grated white pepper and
   nutmeg to taste
Pinch salt

OYSTER LOAVES

Open them, and save the liquor; wash them in it; then strain it through a sieve, and put a little of it into a tosser with a bit of butter and flour, white pepper, a scrape of nutmeg, and a little cream. Stew them, and cut in dice; put them into rolls sold for the purpose.

MRS. RUNDELL
A New System of Domestic Cookery, 1865

Preheat oven to 350 degrees.

Slice off the top quarter of each brioche and scoop out most of the inside with a fork, being careful not to cut through the bottom or sides. (Although the original recipe does not suggest it, I like to melt ¼ cup of butter and brush the insides of the rolls with it.) Replace the top and put the hollow rolls into the oven for 8 to 10 minutes to warm.

Meanwhile, remove the oysters from their liquid, and pass this liquid through a strainer to remove any odd bits of shell. Set aside.

In a saucepan, melt the butter and whisk in the flour until it is well blended. Over low heat, whisk in the heavy cream, ¼ cup of the oyster liquor, and seasonings to taste.

Add the oysters and bring the sauce just to the boil. With a slotted spoon, immediately remove the oysters and dice them, if desired. Immediately fill each brioche shell with the oysters and some of the cream sauce. Replace the top crust and serve at once.

Roast Goose with Sage and Onion Dressing

Makes 8 servings

To have a proper Victorian Christmas feast, you must have roast goose with the classic sage and onion dressing. As the onions are parboiled first, the stuffing is pleasantly mild, and with the addition of apples, it is milder still. Mrs. Beeton, in the Book of Household Management, *suggests adding part of the goose liver (simmered) as an optional addition to the stuffing—a fine idea. Apple or "tomata" sauce are the suggested accompaniments.*

9-pound goose
2 teaspoons coarse salt

FOR THE STUFFING:

3 medium onions, peeled
**4 large apples, peeled, cored and
  chopped (tart cooking apples such
  as Granny Smiths are best)**
**2 tablespoons (or less) loosely
  packed dried sage leaves,
  crumbled**
**½ teaspoon freshly ground black
  pepper**
**1 tablespoon butter, cut into
  tiny bits**
**Garnishes: sliced apples, greens
  such as parsley or watercress**

FOR THE BROWN GRAVY:

**Gizzard, neck, heart, liver and wing
  tips of the goose, chopped**
1 onion, peeled and sliced
1 carrot, sliced
**1-2 tablespoons rendered goose fat
  or cooking oil**
3 cups stock or beef bouillon
½ bay leaf
3 sprigs parsley
Salt and pepper to taste

TO ROAST A GOOSE

After it has been picked and singed with care, put into the body of the goose two parboiled onions of moderate size, finely chopped, and mixed with half an ounce of minced sage-leaves, a saltspoonful of salt, and half as much black pepper, or a proportionate quantity of cayenne; to these add a small slice of fresh butter. Truss the goose, and after it is on the spit, tie it firmly at both ends that it may turn steadily, and that the seasoning may not escape; roast it at a brisk fire, and keep it constantly basted. Serve it with brown gravy, and apple or tomato sauce. When the taste is in favour of a stronger seasoning than the above, which occurs, we apprehend, but seldom, use raw onions for it, and increase the quantity; but should one still milder be preferred, mix a handful of fine bread-crumbs with the other ingredients, or two or three minced apples . . . A teaspoonful of made-mustard, half as much of salt, and a small portion of cayenne, smoothly mixed with a glass of port wine, are sometimes poured into the goose just before it is served, through a cut made in the apron . . .

ELIZA ACTON
Modern Cookery in All its Branches, 1848

FOR THE PORT WINE SAUCE

½ cup port
1 teaspoon mustard
Pinch cayenne pepper
Salt to taste

Preheat oven to 450 degrees.

Rub the goose inside and out with the coarse salt. Set aside.

Parboil the onions in boiling water for 5 minutes. Remove them with a slotted spoon and, when they are cool enough to handle, chop them finely.

In a large bowl, combine the onions, chopped apples, sage, pepper and butter. Just before cooking, place this stuffing in the cavity of the goose. Sew or skewer the openings, and truss the goose in the usual way.

Roast the goose at 450 degrees for the first 15 minutes, then reduce the heat to 350 degrees and turn the goose onto its side. After 1 hour, turn the goose onto its other side. For the final 15 minutes, roast the goose on its back. Baste the goose with about 3 tablespoons of boiling water about every 20 minutes during the whole period of roasting. (Allow about 15 minutes per pound for the total weight of the stuffed goose, or approximately 2½ hours for a 9-pound stuffed goose. When done, the internal temperature should register 180 degrees, the legs should move up and down freely, and the juices should run a pale yellow.)

While the goose is roasting, prepare the gravy. In a large saucepan, brown the goose parts, onion and carrot in the fat. When they are nicely browned, add the stock and seasonings. Simmer, partially covered, for about 1 hour, skimming occasionally. Strain, degrease and pour into a warmed sauce-boat for serving.

For the optional port wine sauce, combine the ingredients in a small saucepan. Just before serving the goose, slit open the breast and pour the sauce on top.

Superlative Mincemeat

Makes 1½ quarts or 2¾ pounds

"Superlative" may sound immodest, but why should Eliza Acton mince words when describing such an outstanding mincemeat recipe? It is a good idea to prepare this mincemeat at least a few days in advance to give the flavors a chance to mingle.

2 large lemons
2 small tart apples, pared, cored
   and grated
2 cups raisins
2 cups dried currants
Generous ¼ cup coarsely chopped
   citron
Generous ¼ cup coarsely chopped
   candied orange peel
2 cups (½ pound) loosely packed
   grated beef kidney suet
1 tablespoon freshly grated nutmeg
½ teaspoon mace
¾ teaspoon ground ginger
1 teaspoon salt
½ cup brandy
¼ pound lean round beef, ground
   (optional; see note)

In a small saucepan, cover the lemons with water. Bring to a boil and simmer for 20 minutes. Remove the lemons, cut them in half and remove the pits. Chop the lemons finely.

In a bowl, combine the remaining ingredients together and mix them very well.

Press the mincemeat into large sterile jars with tight-fitting lids and store them in a cool place until needed. Should the mincemeat at any time seem dry and crumbly, perk it up by stirring in more brandy.

NOTE: This recipe makes enough for 2 8-inch covered pies or about 3 dozen Mince Pies Royal (see following recipe). If you plan to bake the mincemeat in pies or tarts, you will find that adding the meat at the last minute enriches the flavor. If you do this, do not plan on storing the mincemeat for more than a few days in the refrigerator.

Mince Pies Royal

These lovely tartlets, crowned with their golden meringues, are indeed fit for royalty.

1 pound Superlative Mincemeat
   (see preceding recipe)
10 tablespoons sugar
¼ cup lemon juice
Grated rind of 2 lemons
¼ cup clarified butter
8 egg yolks
3 egg whites

FOR THE SHORT CRUST:

2 tablespoons sugar
Scant 2 cups flour
1½ sticks (6 ounces) chilled butter,
   cut into bits
2 tablespoons ice water

MINCE PIES ROYAL (ENTREMETS)

Add to half a pound of good mincemeat an ounce and a half of pounded sugar, the grated rind and the strained juice of a large lemon, one ounce of clarified butter, and the yolks of four eggs; beat these well together, and half fill, or rather more, with the mixture, some pattypans lined with fine paste; put them into a moderate oven, and when the insides are just set, ice them thickly with the whites of the eggs beaten to snow, and mixed quickly at the moment with four heaped tablespoonsful of pounded sugar; set them immediately into the oven again, and bake them of a fine light brown.

   Mincemeat, ½ lb.; sugar, 1½ oz.; rind and juice, 1 large lemon; butter, 1 oz.; yolks, 4 eggs. Icing: whites, 4 eggs; sugar, 4 tablespoonsful.

VERY RICH SHORT CRUST FOR TARTS

Break lightly, with the least possible handling, six ounces of butter into eight of flour; add a dessertspoonful of pounded sugar, and two or three of water; roll the paste for several minutes, to blend the ingredients well, folding it together like puff-crust, and touch it as little as possible.

   Flour, 8 ozs.; butter, 6 ozs; pounded sugar, 1 dessertspoonful; water, 1 to 2 spoonsful.

ELIZA ACTON
Modern Cookery in All its Branches, 1848

Preheat oven to 350 degrees.

In a bowl, combine Superlative Mincemeat with 6 table-spoons of sugar, the lemon juice, lemon rind, clarified butter and egg yolks. Blend well and set aside.

To prepare the crust, combine the flour with the sugar in a bowl or in a food processor. Cut the butter into the flour until the mixture resembles oatmeal. Rapidly blend the ice water into the flour and knead briefly.

Lightly grease 12 tartlet shells. On a lightly floured board, roll out the dough until it is about ¼ inch thick. (You may fold the dough a few times, envelope fashion, as for puff pastry, but this instruction in the original recipe does not seem worth the effort.) Cut out circles and press them into the tartlet shells, making sure to patch up any holes.

Spoon some mincemeat into each shell and bake for 20 minutes. When the filling is set, beat the egg whites with the remaining 4 tablespoons of sugar until stiff. Spread this meringue over each tartlet and bake for 25 minutes longer. Remove the tartlets from the oven and cool them on a rack for about 10 minutes. To remove them from the tins, run a knife along the edges and gently pry them out.

Christmas Pudding

Makes a 3-pound round pudding (8 small servings)

To think of English Christmas is to picture a Christmas pudding being presented at the table in all its blazing glory. It is hard to believe that the sweet and pack-a-wallop Christmas pudding was at one time served as a first course, but that seems to have been the custom during at least part of the 18th century: "No man of the most rigid Virtue gives offence by an excess in plum-pudding or plum-porridge, because they are the first parts of the dinner," claims Addison in the Tatler.

The practice of boiling a pudding in a cloth no doubt grew out of the old convenient habit of cooking gruels enclosed in an animal's stomach, and it is still a very practical way to cook—provided you have a cotton cloth about 15 inches square, some string, and a big pot for the boiling.

Some puddings were so large that they were boiled in the same huge copper used to heat the water for the weekly wash, hence the description in Dickens's A Christmas Carol: *"Hallo! A great deal of steam! The pudding was out of the copper. A smell like a washing-day! That was the cloth. A smell like an eating-house and a pastry-cook's next door to each other, with a laundress's next door to that! That was the pudding!"*

The pudding usually was first cooked five weeks before Christmas on Stir-up Sunday. This name originally came from the first line of the Collect for that day which began, "Stir up, we beseech thee, O Lord, the wills of thy faithful people," but for good luck it was considered essential for each member of the family to "stir up" the pudding mixture before the cooking began.

This pudding is delicious right out of the pot, warm, after its first 3½-hour boiling. But you might prefer to make it a few months (or a year?) in advance and store it in a cool place so that the flavors have a chance to settle down together. If you choose the latter approach, then tie the pudding back in the cloth and boil it an additional 2 hours before serving.

½ cup flour
1 cup dry breadcrumbs
2 cups (½ pound loosely packed) grated beef kidney suet
1 cup (tightly packed) raisins
1¼ cups currants
1 cup peeled, minced apples
⅓ cup coarsely chopped candied orange peel
¾ cup sugar
⅛ teaspoon salt
Scant ½ teaspoon freshly grated nutmeg
⅛ teaspoon mace
¼ cup good quality brandy
3 large eggs, lightly beaten
Punch Sauce (see next recipe)

In a very large bowl, combine all of the above ingredients. Blend them well.

Wet the pudding cloth thoroughly and sprinkle it generously with flour. With your fingers, spread out the flour to form a thin layer on the cloth. Set the pudding cloth into a medium-sized bowl, pressing it into the shape of the bowl. Set the mixture into the cloth and tie it tightly about an inch above the bulge of the mixture (allowing the pudding room to swell).

Bring a very large pot of water to the boil. Gently set the pudding into the water and bring the water back to the boil. Then reduce the heat to medium so that the water boils gently for 3½ hours, replacing water as needed so that the pudding is always totally submerged. Occasionally lift the pudding so that it doesn't stick to the bottom of the pot.

When the pudding is done, lift it up and place it in a large colander to drain. When it is cool enough to handle, gently remove the string and the cloth. (If you are not planning to

78 / CHRISTMAS FEASTS

use the pudding immediately, let it cool completely, wrap it thoroughly in a few layers of aluminum foil and store it in a cool place until needed.)

To serve the pudding, set it on a platter, spoon some warmed brandy on top (if desired) and hold a match nearby until it catches. You may, of course, set a sprig of holly in the center for good luck. Serve warm with a sauceboat of punch sauce on the side.

CHRISTMAS PUDDING

To three ounces of flour, and the same weight of fine, lightly-grated bread-crumbs, add six of beef kidney-suet, chopped small, six of raisins weighed after they are stoned, six of well cleaned currants, four ounces of minced apples, five of sugar, two of candied orange-rind, half a teaspoonful of nutmeg mixed with pounded mace, a very little salt, a small glass of brandy, and three whole eggs. Mix and beat these ingredients well together, tie them tightly in a thickly floured cloth, and boil them for three hours and a half. We can recommend this as a remarkably light small rich pudding: it may be served with German, wine, or punch sauce.

Flour, 3 ozs.; bread-crumbs, 3 ozs.; suet, stoned raisins, and currants, each, 6 ozs.; minced apples, 4 ozs.; sugar, 5 ozs.; candied peel, 2 ozs.; spice, ½ teaspoonful; salt, few grains; brandy, small wineglassfull; eggs, 3: 3½ hours.

ELIZA ACTON
Modern Cookery in All its Branches, 1848

Punch Sauce

This smooth and flavorful punch sauce is one which Eliza Acton recommends to accompany plum pudding. You may prepare it a few hours in advance, refrigerate it, and then reheat it just before serving.

Scant ⅓ cup sugar
¾ cup water
½ small lemon
⅓ juice orange
3 tablespoons butter, cut into bits
1 teaspoon flour
¼ cup brandy
¼ cup white wine
⅓ cup rum

In a small heavy pot, dissolve the sugar in the water.

Meanwhile, squeeze the lemon and orange and reserve the juices. Chop the peels into 3 or 4 pieces and place them in the sugar syrup. Boil gently for about 20 minutes. Press them against the side of the pot to squeeze out all the flavor, and remove the peels with a slotted spoon. (You may reserve them for use as candied peel.)

Place the butter in a small bowl and sprinkle it with the flour. Mash them together until the flour is completely absorbed.

Whisk the butter mixture into the sugar syrup over medium heat. Add the reserved fruit juices, brandy, wine and rum and heat just to the boiling point, but do not boil once the spirits have been added.

Serve very hot, or store (after it has cooled) in the refrigerator, covered with a piece of waxed paper until needed. Then reheat and serve in a sauceboat.

PUNCH SAUCE FOR SWEET PUDDINGS

This is a favourite sauce with custard, plain bread, and plum-puddings. With two ounces of sugar and a quarter-pint of water, boil very gently the rind of half a small lemon, and somewhat less of orange-peel, from fifteen to twenty minutes; strain out the rinds, thicken the sauce with an ounce and a half of butter and nearly a teaspoonful of flour, add a half-glass of brandy, the same of white wine, two thirds of a glass of rum, with the juice of half an orange, and rather less of lemon-juice: serve the sauce very hot, but do not allow it to boil after the spirit is stirred in.

Sugar, 2 ozs.; water, ¼ pint; lemon and orange rind: 14 to 20 minutes. Butter, 1½ oz.; flour, 1 teaspoonful; brandy and white wine each ½ wineglassful; rum, two thirds of glassful; orange and lemon juice.

ELIZA ACTON
Modern Cookery in All its Branches, 1848

Shrub

Serves 6

This odd-sounding word comes from the Arabic shurb, *meaning drink. Apparently, it was a popular beverage among the ladies (it is dangerously pleasant to drink), as Dickens indicates in* Sketches by Boz: "Miss Ivin's friend's young man would have the ladies go into the Crown, to taste some shrub."*

The original recipe suggests preparing the drink at least five days in advance. If that is not possible, you will find you have quite a tasty punch almost immediately after you do the mixing. It is likely that oranges were less sweet in those days, and you may wish to reduce the amount of sugar in this recipe.

5-6 juice oranges
2 cups (or less) sugar
1 quart rum or brandy

Squeeze the oranges until you have 2 cups of juice. Reserve half of the skins. Strain the juice to remove the pith and pits.

Combine the juice, sugar and liquor in a large bottle. Coarsely chop the orange peels and add them. Cover and shake the mixture.

About 8 hours later, strain out the peels. Cover and shake the mixture about 4 times daily for the next 4 days. Reserve for use.

To serve, pour into a small punch bowl and chill with ice either in the bowl or in individual glasses.

NOTES AND SUGGESTIONS FOR FURTHER READING

◉

A ROMAN SATURNALIA BANQUET

1. See Apicius, *The Roman Cookery Book,* translated by Barbara Flower and Elisabeth Rosenbaum (London: Harrap, 1974), p. 99. All recipe translations have been taken from this edition.
2. The most accessible copy of this text is the Flower and Rosenbaum translation mentioned above. Although difficult to find, copies may usually be ordered from The Wine and Food Library, 1207 W. Madison, Ann Arbor, MI 48103.

Two books are particularly likely to entertain you on the subject of Roman banqueting. They are Suetonius's *The Twelve Caesars* and Petronius's *The Satyricon* (see especially the chapter called "Dinner with Trimalchio"). Both are available in Harvard's Loeb Classical Library series and in Penguin paperbacks. Additional background material and adapted recipes may be found in *Ancient Roman Feasts and Recipes* by Jon and Julia Solomon (Miami: E.A. Seemann, 1977), though, unfortunately, the original recipes are not quoted.

A MEDIEVAL CHRISTMAS FEAST

1. W.F. Dawson, *Christmas: Its Origin and Associations* (London: Elliot Stock, 1902; repr. Detroit: Gale Research Co., 1968), p. 13.
2. Gillian Edwards, *Hogmanay & Tiffany* (London: Geoffrey Bles, 1970), p. 21
3. *Oxford English Dictionary;* see entry under "wassail."
4. J.R.R. Tolkien and E.V. Gordon, eds., *Sir Gawain and the Green Knight* (Oxford: Clarendon Press, 1970), l. 45; modernization my own.
5. John Russell, *The Boke of Nurture* in F.J. Furnivall, ed., *Early English Meals and Manners.* Early English Text Society (OS) 32 (London: Oxford Univ. Press, 1868), pp. 48-50.
6. Quoted in John Ashton, *A Righte Merrie Christmasse!* (New York: Benjamin Blom, 1968), p. 12.
7. See Furnivall, ed., *op. cit.,* pp. 178-81. Modernization my own.

Those who wish further background on medieval cookery will enjoy Bridget Henisch's *Fast and Feast: Food in Medieval Society* (University Park: Pennsylvania State Univ. Press, 1976). Additional medieval recipes adapted to modern cookery may be found in my own *To the King's Taste* (New York: Metropolitan Museum of Art, 1975). My edition of the complete text of the manuscript cookbook, *The Fourme of Cury* (c. 1390), will be published shortly by Garland Press in New York. An edition of the Harleian Manuscripts has been done by Thomas Austin, *Two Fifteenth-Century Cookery Books,* Early English Text Society (OS) 91 (London: Oxford Univ. Press, 1888; reprinted 1964).

A 17TH-CENTURY CHRISTMAS BANQUET

1. W.F. Dawson, *Christmas: Its Origin and Associations* (London: Elliot Stock, 1902; repr. Detroit: Gale Research Co., 1968), p. 199. Unless otherwise noted, subsequent quotations in this chapter have been taken from this volume, pp. 119-216.
2. Quoted in Michael Harrison, *The Story of Christmas* (London: Odhams Press, Ltd., 1951), p. 144.
3. This recipe may be found in *A Closet for Ladies and Gentlewomen* (London, 1608).
4. The fork fought a long battle for acceptance in England and was by no means universally used during the 17th century. "As for us in the country," claimed Nicholas Breton in 1618, "when we have washed our hands after no foul work, nor handling any unwholesome thing, we need no little forks to make hay with our mouths, to throw our meat into them." See *Inedited Tracts* by The Roxburghe Library (London, 1868), p. 201.
5. An edited text of this manuscript has been published by Catherine Frere (Cambridge: Cambridge Univ. Press, 1913).

Those who wish further background on cookery of this period will enjoy Madge Lorwin's *Dining with William Shakespeare* (New York: Atheneum, 1976), which includes a wide variety of recipes adapted for modern cookery. Additional adapted recipes and lore may be found in my own *To the Queen's Taste* (New York: Metropolitan Museum of Art, 1976). An excellent source for general background on the uses of food through history is C. Anne Wilson's *Food and Drink in Britain* (London: Constable, 1973).

CHRISTMAS IN THE PUDDING AGE

1. John Ashton, *A Righte Merrie Christmasse!* (New York: Benjamin Blom, 1968), p. 176.
2. W.F. Dawson, *Christmas: Its Origins and Associations* (London: Elliot Stock, 1902; repr. Detroit: Gale Research Co., 1968), p. 227.
3. Quoted in Dawson, p. 232.

Those who wish further background on cookery of this period may wish to consult my own *Dinner with Tom Jones* (New York: Metropolitan Museum of Art, 1977). There is a delightful chapter on "Minc'd Pies and Plum-Porridge" in *Hogmanay & Tiffany* by Gillian Edwards (London: Geoffrey Bles, 1970).

A VICTORIAN CHRISTMAS DINNER

1. Quoted in Michael Harrison, *The Story of Christmas* (London: Odhams Press, Ltd., 1951), p. 174.
2. Quoted in John Ashton, *A Righte Merrie Christmasse!* (New York: Benjamin Blom, 1968), p. 87.

3. Quoted in Gerard Brett, *Dinner is Served* (Hamden, Conn.: Archon, 1969), p. 130

Those who enjoy reading about the Victorian period will take pleasure in Antony Miall's *The Victorian Christmas Book* (New York: Pantheon, 1978). It is generously illustrated with period engravings, most of which, unfortunately, are unidentified. The recipes from Eliza Acton's *Modern Cookery* used in this chapter are from the American edition revised by Mrs. S.J. Hale (Philadelphia: Lea and Blanchard, 1848).

ILLUSTRATIONS

Unless otherwise indicated, all illustrations are from The Metropolitan Museum of Art.

Title page: Ink and watercolor design for frontispiece to *The Story of Peter Poodle*, by Will Bradley, 1906. Gift of Fern Bradley Dufner (52.625.126). **8** Illustration from *A Philosophical . . . History . . . of Inebriating Liquors and Other Stimulants* by Samuel Morewood. Dublin, 1838. The Bettmann Archive. **14** Bronze cauldron. Etruscan, early 7th century B.C. Purchase, 1954, Joseph Pulitzer Bequest (54.11.1). **21** Marble relief representing wine shop. Roman, Imperial Period. Fletcher Fund (25.78.63). **64** Wood engraving from *The Christmas Box*. London, 1829. Anonymous Gift (41.102.1). **79** "Christmas Pudding." Illustration by Robert Seymour from Thomas Kibble Hervey's *The Book of Christmas*. London, 1837. Courtesy of The Newberry Library, Chicago.

All below: Harris Brisbane Dick Fund.
13 Engraving by Agostino Veneziano. Italian, 16th century. (26.50.1[38]). **26** Woodcut from *Der Spiegel der Menschen Behaltnis*. Speyer, 1479-81. (31.53[38]). **33** Woodcut from *Kalendar deutsch*. Augsburg, 1484. (26.56.1). **35** Woodcut from Petrus de Crescentius' *Das buch von pflantzung der acker, Boum und aller Kruter*. Strasbourg, 1512. (26.100.2). **36** Detail of engraving by Abraham Bosse. French, 17th century. (26.49.34). **51** "Wassail." Woodcut by Joseph Crawhall from *Crawhall's Chap-book Chaplets*. London, 1883. (840 ref.). **62** Illustration by Randolph Caldecott from Washington Irving's *Old Christmas*. London, 1878. (17.3.2641-41). **68** "New-Year's Calls—The Knickerbockers of . . . 1873." Detail of wood engraving after Solomon Eytinge from *Harper's Weekly*, January 4, 1873. (29.88.9[13]). **74** Illustration by Randolph Caldecott from Washington Irv-ing's *Old Christmas*. London, 1878. (17.3.2641-41). **76** "The Christmas-Tree." Wood engraving after John W. Ehninger from *Harper's Bazar*, January 1, 1870. (33.21.8[28]). **77** "The Christmas-Tree." Wood engraving after Winslow Homer from *Harper's Weekly*, December 25, 1858. (36.13.5[2]). **81** Illustration by Randolph Caldecott from Washington Irving's *Old Christmas*. London, 1878. (17.3.2641-41). **84** "Kitchen Staff." Drawing by John Leech. British, 19th century. (7.97.12).

All below: The Elisha Whittelsey Collection. The Elisha Whittelsey Fund.
29 Woodcut from Remy Dupuys' *La Tryumphante et solemnelle entree . . . de . . . Charles prince des hespaignes . . . en sa ville de Bruges*. Paris, about 1515. (49.71.2). **40** "December." Engraving by Crispin de Passe after Marten de Vos. Dutch, 17th century. (49.95.1539). **43** Detail of engraving after David Vinckeboons. Dutch, 17th century. (57.630.6). **45** Costume symbolizing the trade of a rotisseur. Etching and engraving after Nicholas de Larmessin. French, 1690. (49.70.64). **47** Detail of engraving by Jacob Matham after Pieter Aertsen. Dutch, 1603. (49.95.803). **48** "September." Engraving by C.V. Dalen after Joachim Sandrart. Dutch, 17th century. (55.565.51). **50** Detail of engraving from *Lo Scalco alla Moderna* by Antonio Latini. Naples, 1694. (49.42.3). **67** Etching by Thomas Rowlandson from his *Outlines of Figures, Landscapes, & Cattle . . . .* London, 1790-92. (59.533.1017).

All below: Gift of Juliet W. Robinson.
52 "The Coachman mixes a Christmas Bowl." Illustration by Randolph Caldecott from *Gleanings from the "Graphic"*. London, 1889. (18.77). **58** "Christmas Visitors." Illustration by Randolph Caldecott from *Gleanings from*

the *"Graphic"*. London, 1889. (18.77). **66** "The Christmas Wine." Illustration by Randolph Caldecott from *Gleanings from the "Graphic"*. London, 1889. (18.77)

All below: Rogers Fund.
17 Marble relief representing funerary banquet. Roman, 69-96 A.D. (27.122.2). **18** Bronze ladle. Etruscan, late 5th century B.C. (21.88.69). **19** Silver spoons. Roman, Imperial Period. (20.49.6,7). **22** Woodcut by Michael Wolgemuth from *Der Schatzbehalter*. Nuremberg, 1491. (19.49.4). **31** Woodcut from *Kuchenmeisterei*. Augsburg, 1507. **57** Wood engraving by William J. Linton after Harry Fenn from John Greenleaf Whittier's *Snow Bound*. Boston, 1869. (19.44.34).

IRENA CHALMERS COOKBOOKS, INC.

Editorial Offices
23 East 92nd Street
New York, NY 10028
(212) 289-3105

Sales Offices
P.O. Box 322
Brown Summit, NC 27214
(800) 334-8128

Publisher
Irena Chalmers

Managing Editor
Jean Atcheson

Sales and Marketing Director
Diane J. Kidd

The Great American Cooking Schools
Series Design
Helene Berinsky

Cover Design
Milton Glaser
Karen Skelton, *Associate Designer*

Cover Photography
Matthew Klein

Typesetting
J&J Graphics, Greensboro, NC

Printing
Lucas Litho, Inc., Baltimore, MD

Editor for Christmas Feasts
Jean Atcheson

Art Director
Mary Ann Joulwan

Picture Research
Alden Rockwell
Special Publications
The Metropolitan Museum of Art

Cover Design for
Metropolitan Museum edition
Peter Oldenburg